THE TAO OF BOOK PUBLICITY:
A BEGINNER'S GUIDE TO BOOK PROMOTION

By Paula Margulies

The Tao of Book Publicity: A Beginner's Guide to Book
Promotion
by Paula Margulies

Cover art: Troy O'Brien
Author photo: Lisa K. Miller

ISBN 13: 978-0-9913545-3-5
ISBN 10: 0-9913545-3-2

One People Press, 8145 Borzoi Way, San Diego, CA 92129
Manufactured in the United States of America

For my clients and students,
who have always been my best teachers

TABLE OF CONTENTS

CHAPTER 1. WHERE DO I BEGIN?

If you've picked up this book, you're more than likely a beginning author who is writing a book, or someone who has just finished writing one. If so, congratulations! Writing is a worthy art, and finishing a book is a great accomplishment.

For many beginning writers, the thought of having to market their books can be terrifying, or in the best circumstances, a mystery. "What should I do first?" they ask. "Where do I start? Do I need to think about marketing before my book is ready to launch? How much will it cost to promote my book? What is the best way to promote it?"

I hear these questions often from authors who contact me about publicity services. Many authors don't know what they want in the way of publicity, but they know they need to do some amount of marketing and publicity in order to sell their books.

This book answers some of the questions I've heard from authors in the course of my thirty-plus-year career as a book publicist. I've tried to organize each chapter in a logical sequence so that those topics that an author needs to address first appear early on, although there are some topics that can be important at both the end and the beginning--or even during--a book's marketing life.

As you read this book, please remember that some of the topics discussed in these chapters will apply to you and your book, and some will not. Likewise, some of the advice regarding scheduling, budget, strategy, etc., may sound good to you, while some of it may not; book publicity is not a one-size-fits-all proposition.

My suggestion is to read each chapter (in any order you like--they are designed to read as stand-alone units) and see what sounds as if it might be a good fit for you and your book. If something doesn't sound right to you, ignore it. The information listed in these chapters is here to help guide you and provide some insight into what I believe are the common practices of most book publicists, but none of what's here is meant to be a hard-and-fast prescription for your own individual book publicity plans.

Rather, these chapters outline what I do in my business when I provide publicity services for my clients. The topics covered here contain information that has been honed after years of successful public relations work for fiction and nonfiction authors, and I offer it here to provide ideas about how you might want to publicize your book, or to help illuminate and illustrate those aspects of book publicity that you want to understand better.

So, let's begin.

CHAPTER 2. THE TAO OF BOOK PUBLICITY

Of all the books I've kept on the nightstand next to my bed, there are two that stand out as mainstays over the years. One is *Walden*, by Henry David Thoreau. I am perpetually fascinated by the simple truths--self-reliance, economy, and simplicity--described in those pages, and I find myself going back to them often for inspiration and guidance.

The other book that has provided years of inspirational nighttime reading is the Stephen Mitchell translation of Lao Tzu's *Tao Te Ching*. Written during the sixth century BC by the sage Laozi (or Lao Tzu, "Old Master"), a record-keeper in the Zhou Dynasty court, the eighty-one poems that make up the book comprise an instructional guide for everything from politics and governance to practical wisdom and tips for self-knowledge. The concepts have to do with developing humility, compassion, and moderation in how we govern ourselves and others, including learning to yield when the chips are down. Rather than pursuing desire, the Tao emphasizes being willing to step back, listen, and operate from a central place of quiet certainty. In the world of the Tao, those who are stubborn and rigid in their beliefs will suffer, while those who remain open and flexible prevail.

While perusing the Tao, I am often struck by how much of its simple wisdom applies to book publicity. Many authors find the marketing side of publishing crass and stressful, but there are aspects

3

of promotion that can be explained and illuminated by some of the principles in the Tao. Here are a few that seem to apply:

12
The Master observes the world
but trusts his inner vision.
He allows things to come and go.
His heart is open as the sky.

Most of the authors I work with come to me for one of three reasons: they know what to do, but don't have the time to promote their work themselves; they don't know what to do and would like some help; or they've already tried to promote their books, but have not had much success. My first suggestion in all these cases is that these authors take a moment to observe what is happening with their genre and target market, and then sit quietly and consider what it is they want in the way of promotion. I ask them to decide what sales numbers they hope to achieve, what kinds of publicity they'd like (media interviews? book tours? speaking tours? reviews?), and finally, how much they're willing to spend toward making those goals a reality. Authors have to be comfortable with what we're doing as a team and how much they're spending on their publicity programs, and they also have to have some level of trust with what I'm recommending for them. The clients who end up having the most success are often those who listen to suggestions about how to proceed, embrace the process we agree to undertake, and open their hearts to new ideas and ways of doing things.

56
Those who know don't talk.
Those who talk don't know.

Those who contact me and want to tell me that they already know everything there is to know about book promotion and publicity are often, ironically, authors who have never published a book before, or who have tried it and have not had any success. But those who are willing to admit that they don't know much about the process, and who listen to and trust their publicist's expertise, are generally more successful than their all-knowing brethren. Why? Because the business of PR, strangely enough, comes from a place of not-knowing. We have no guarantees that producers or acquisitions editors will like our pitch, nor can we strong-arm them into accepting it. All we can do is use our established connections and relationships, our experience, and the knowledge at hand to make the best pitch we can. Likewise, we can make educated guesses about the target readership for a book and where that readership exists, but there are no guarantees that after we reach them, the readers will buy. With publicity, the best we can do is put our work out there and trust that our publicity contacts and knowledge will open the path and allow the right exposure to happen.

Those who claim to already know it all are often surprised at this; they mistakenly believe that there is a magic formula (a certain number of radio appearances, a certain kind of media list) that will make their sales suddenly skyrocket. That kind of magical result usually doesn't occur; in most cases, it is the authors who take careful, steady, well-planned steps toward reaching their audiences who will ultimately achieve a desirable level of awareness for themselves and their books.

64
Rushing into action, you fail.
Trying to grasp things, you lose them.
Forcing a project to completion,
you ruin what was almost ripe.

I receive a lot of books from potential clients and so many of them are, sadly, not ready for public consumption. As the Tao suggests, rushing a piece of writing to market without the proper preparation, revision, editing, and packaging, can be a recipe for failure. Better for authors to allow adequate time for writing projects to develop and flourish, giving them the experienced, professional polishing and packaging they require before releasing them to the world.

68
Act without doing;
work without effort.
Think of the small as large
and the few as many.

Confront the difficult
while it is still easy;
accomplish the great task
by a series of small acts.

Making the long journey of book promotion a successful one by breaking it up into small steps is wise advice for authors when they begin work with a publicist. At first, starting out can seem overwhelming, but there is a system to promoting a person's work. Initially, we plan our strategy: we define the audience we're targeting, we create lists of places where those targeted readers can be found, and we map out our next steps, including setting up book and blog tours, scheduling speaking appearances, contacting media, sending out books for review, etc. We develop media kits, including press releases, author and cover photos, Q&A's, and more. We place the releases on the news wires, we work with our established contacts, we develop a schedule, and we move forward, knowing that this series of small steps will eventually help us to complete our journey and accomplish the great task of allowing the author's work to become known.

CHAPTER 3. THOUGHTS ON WRITING AND EDITING

As a book publicist and an avid reader, my first word of advice to those who contact me regarding my services is to write the best books they possibly can. Every year, I'm sent books by hundreds of authors looking for promotional help, but since I only handle two or three clients at a time, I tend to be choosy about whom I agree to represent.

Judging writing is a subjective art, and I try to be fair with every book I receive. Instead of asking whether or not I love the book (something I've heard a few agents say they must feel before they take on a client), I ask myself, *Can I sell it?* This is a bit of a different question--my concern is not whether the book is great fiction or nonfiction, but more whether booksellers, reporters, and media producers will be interested in it when I call to give them a pitch.

Even so, if a book is poorly written or riddled with typos and grammatical errors, it isn't likely that I'll be able to place it anywhere, even if it has a great topic. Likewise if the title is off-putting or the cover art is somehow wrong for the book or its audience. A young adult (YA) novel, for example, with a Goth title and violent cover art may fly with the kids it's designed to reach, but it won't get past librarians or teachers who are the gatekeepers that decide whether or not a YA book can appear at a library or school.

Every writer should have as many people as possible, including a professional copyeditor, read a book before it goes to an agent, editor, or publicist. Best case, authors should first revise and rewrite with a high-caliber writing group. After rounds of testing with other authors, the book should then go through a good edit, with a *paid* professional copyeditor, rather than a family member or friend (unfortunately, those who know the author closely too often cannot get past their relationship biases when judging a friend or family member's work).

I'm seeing more self-published work lately and many of those books, though interesting and decently written, have not had an agent or editor to help with the conceptual issues and editorial corrections that most books need. Although it's tough to get an agent these days, and even tougher to be published by a larger press, the value those entities bring to an author's work is immeasurable. I know this from experience--before shopping my debut novel to publishing houses, my first agent worked with me for four months, offering input on what was missing and urging me to write seven new scenes for the book. Some agents give thorough critiques and mark-ups of manuscripts; others will work with authors for months or even years, making certain that a book is the best it can be before it reaches an editor at a publishing house.

And editors, despite being overworked and beleaguered by cut-backs and mergers, will put their own spin on a text. Some do more than others but, in most cases, a book will have gone through many rounds of revision and polishing before it hits the market if published by a larger house or even a diligent small press.

Can authors with self-published books get the same quality end-product without agents and editors? Certainly, although the onus will be on the authors to provide editorial and packaging resources for themselves, which can be expensive or time-consuming, and sometimes both. Many authors, in their hurry to get their books out, forgo these steps and, sadly, the books don't sell.

The bottom line is that, self-published or not, if you want your book to be well-received by booksellers and the media, you must take the time to carefully edit, polish, and package it well.

CHAPTER 4. WHAT EXACTLY IS AN AUTHOR PLATFORM?

Authors often ask me what is meant by the term "platform." Simply put, your platform is all about *you*--the experience, background, and expertise *you* bring to the table, in addition to the wonderful book you've written.

The concept of platform is important when selling a book because it's what the media, especially radio and TV folks, are most interested in when it comes time to set up promotional appearances. I once had a radio producer in New York tell me, "Paula, I don't give a damn about this author's book; I want to know about his background and experience. If he doesn't interest me, his book never will." This may sound a bit harsh, but it's all too true in the world of publicity. If you want premium exposure for your book through traditional radio and TV, *you* are going to be the story.

And it should be a good one. Media producers expect authors to be knowledgeable or experienced in their subject matter, whether the book is nonfiction or fiction. If you have a compelling personal history, expertise in the industry you've written about, or an interesting angle to bring to the interview, then you're more likely to get a *yes* nod from a producer trying to fill a radio or TV time slot. Reporters and producers look for individuals who are unique, compelling, and entertaining as interview subjects. If you're a celebrity or have notoriety in your field, the pathway will be easier. But if not, you've got to develop a platform that will intrigue members of the media if you want to get maximum exposure for your work.

So, how do you go about building your platform? Many authors write about subjects that fascinate them, but they don't always have expertise in those areas. When this is the case, I recommend the following:

1. Teach or give lectures, presentations, and workshops on the topic, even if it's one you only know through research.
2. Keep a list of the presentations you give, and include them in your bio.
3. Get testimonials from the organizers and attendees at your talks and print them on all of your promotional material, including your website.
4. If you haven't yet done so, create a website and an author blog for your book and update both regularly with current information.
5. Follow other blogs in your subject area and comment on them. List your website and blog URLs when you write comments, and develop relationships with bloggers and blog readers in your subject area.
6. Use your blog posts as starting points for articles that you can then send to established websites, blogs, and trade publications.
7. Offer to become a guest blogger or reviewer on other sites, and invite experts in your subject area to guest write for your blog and website.

8. Become active on social media. Establish Facebook, Twitter, Goodreads, and other social media pages, and friend or follow people who might be potential readers or fellow experts in your field. Post often, so that you develop a following for the information you're providing; this will help establish you as an expert. And don't forget to develop relationships with your followers by being friendly and responsive.

9. Make connections with experts in your subject area and ask them to endorse you and your book.

10. Demonstrate your passion for your subject when you speak about it. Know recent statistics and be able to talk about new research or events relevant to your subject area.

11. Develop an up-to-date curriculum vitae (c.v.) that lists all your accomplishments and achievements and demonstrates how well you know your subject area.

Many authors are lucky to have agents who understand the importance of platform and are willing to help them develop the items listed above. But self-published authors, or others who don't have agents, may need to do some of the development work on their own.

Take a look at your platform, and if it needs developing, get going on building it, one step at a time.

CHAPTER 5: ADVICE ON BOOK COVERS
A Word about Front Covers

In the world of book sales, that first impression--
when a reader first sees your book, either on a
bookstore shelf, on a table at an author event, or on
a web page--is a crucial moment in a reader's
buying decision. You want your cover to be
striking, original, and suited to your genre, in order
to make readers willing to take a look at what's
under the cover.

For this reason, book covers must be professionally
designed. I know a lot of authors who argue that
their design skills are good enough to warrant
creating their own covers, but in my thirty-plus
years as a book publicist, I have always been able to
spot the home-designed covers--and if I can spot
them, then readers can, too.

So, what should authors consider when it comes
time to have their covers designed? Here are a few
tips, based on my own experience working with
hundreds of authors' books over the years:

1. Hire a professional designer to create your book cover

Authors really can't skimp on this part--only a
professional can give your book the polished look
that is required in these days of highly competitive
book sales. Your designer should be someone
experienced (look for someone who has a number
of sample covers to show you) and familiar with

covers in your genre. The designer doesn't have to be expensive; I've worked with many professionals over the years who charge a couple of hundred dollars to produce a cover. But take your time when looking for a design professional--note cover designs that catch your eye as you peruse other books, ask writing colleagues for recommendations, and, when you find a designer, ask for references and check them to see what it's like to work with that person.

2. Know what you want in a design

Remember that when you go to sell a book, it will always be judged by readers in terms of the other books out there that compete with it. So, it's important for you to spend some time looking at other books in your book's category or genre, so that you can get a feel for what readers are seeing when they go to buy. Knowing what's typical or appropriate in your category or genre will make it easier for you to work with your designer on what you feel is the best approach for your book. That said, be aware that a professional designer may make recommendations or come up with designs that you hadn't considered before. Be open to your professional's advice, and work together to come up with the most powerful and polished design you can for your book cover.

3. **Your cover will be created as a single (front) page and as a full spread**
Your cover designer will prepare a number of pieces of art for you. The options include the following:

-A JPEG of the front cover--this format will be required for your publicist, or for you yourself, to upload to webpages and social media sites and to send to media outlets (this is the preferred format for most media outlets)

-A PDF of the front cover--this format may be required for uploading to sales platforms like Amazon.com

-A JPEG of the full spread (front, back, and spine) of your book cover--this format will be required for some sales platforms

-A PDF of the full spread (front, back, and spine) of your book cover--this format will be required for some sales platforms

Once you have decided on the final front cover page and full spread artwork for your book cover, you should always be sure to ask your designer for both low resolution (sometimes referred to as "low res") and high resolution ("high res") versions of them. You will use these to fulfill media requests for both versions.

A Word about Back Covers

I was dismayed recently to receive a number of
books from prospective clients (including three
from a small press) that had nothing on the back
covers other than the Bookland EAN barcode and a
brief paragraph about the book.

That's it? A bar code and a paragraph?

Some of these back cover paragraphs were poorly
written and riddled with typos. One included a glib
attempt by the author to downplay his writing skills
with self-effacing humor. One had no description of
the book, but instead listed a sixteen-line quote by a
reviewer. Another filled the entire space of the back
cover in an illegible, shadowed font.

It's hard to believe that in today's crowded market,
authors willingly choose to ignore the valuable
marketing space on their books' back covers.
Because that's what a back cover is--an opportunity
to sell your book to a potential reader. But in order
to sell, the back cover must be professional in
design and compelling in its content.

Here's what I like to see on a back cover (in
addition to the barcode), preferably in this order:

**1. An intriguing, well-written one- or two-
paragraph summary about the book**
If the book is fiction, think of the summary
paragraph as your chance to hook your prospective

reader. Focus on the meat of the story: WHO has to do WHAT to cause WHAT to happen or not happen? Then add details that will appeal to your target audience.

If you're writing nonfiction, describe your book's contents in a way that sets you apart from any other books on the topic. What makes your book different? What special expertise do you bring to the subject matter that will entice readers? And what will readers learn after reading your book?

When you write your back cover copy, think about what your reader is looking for. Describe the story-- or in the case of nonfiction, the book's content--in such a way that the person reading it feels compelled to open the book.

2. At least three one- or two-sentence blurbs from reviewers your target readers will recognize and respect
The more well-known your reviewers, the more likely readers are going to want to take a look at what's inside your book. Network with your friends and fellow authors to locate reviewers who will appeal to your target audience. Send the reviewers copies of your manuscript and ask them to write a blurb for you. When you receive the blurbs, parse them down to one or two sentences that do the best job of relaying what's good about your book. Remember that endorsements are especially important to media folks, so it's worth the time and

effort to try to obtain blurbs from readers who are well-known.

What if you don't know any big names who can endorse your book? Ask your writing group members, fellow authors, friends, and even family members if they'll read your work and give you an endorsement. Choose people who are good representative readers, or those who will give you a well-written, pithy quote. A good review from a reader who represents your book's target audience may be the deciding factor in motivating an interested reader to open and buy the book.

3. A headshot and bio

Readers like to know something about the authors of the books they might buy. By providing a thumbnail-sized photo of yourself, and a brief, one-paragraph bio, you are using yourself as a selling point. Be sure your headshot is professional-looking, and include the most important facts about yourself and your platform in the bio. Also, list your website and other social media sites where readers can find more information about you.

Your headshot should appear next to the biographical paragraph and should be small enough to fit the space next to the bio, but large enough that your features are recognizable.

In addition to the bar code and pricing information, you may want to include listing the book's subject category (usually this appears in the upper left-hand corner of the back cover). Doing so helps staff members at bookstores and libraries know where to shelve your book.

Finally, think of your back cover as prime advertising space and use as much of it as you can, with proper attention to design and legibility. If you have won awards, be sure to list those on the back cover as well. But most important, design your back cover so it inspires your readers to buy. Give them a glimpse of your voice and style with an intriguing, well-written synopsis. Let them know that your work is important and endorsed by others with a few positive blurbs. And introduce yourself and your platform by including an author photo and a brief bio.

Chapter 6. Timing

To everything, there is a season, and after many years of helping authors publicize their work, I've learned that some seasons are better than others for certain aspects of book promotion. Here are my recommendations on timing for book publicity, whether you are traditionally or self-published with ebooks or print versions or both, including a breakdown by the specific media and venues to be approached (please note this is general advice based on my experience as a publicist; your experiences may be different, depending on the kind of book you've written):

1. The best time to promote a new book: the first six to eight months after its release
The first six to eight months that a book is out is the best time period to promote it, because that is when authors are most likely to receive yes nods from booksellers and members of the media for signings and interviews (except for those topics that tie in with breaking or hot news topics--then an older book can be considered timely). When I work with new clients, I tell them to plan on spending the majority of their promotional time, travel, and budget during the first six months after release; after that, I recommend they get back to work on their next books.

2. The best time for book signings and tours: spring, summer, and early fall
Booksellers are more apt to say yes to signings in the spring, summer, and early fall, especially in

those areas of the country where winter weather might be an issue. Also, most bookstores don't want to host authors during the holidays; they have enough traffic in their stores at that time. And many of them don't begin to set event dates on their calendars until after the start of the new year.

3. When to begin calls to book spring, summer, and early fall signing tours: January to March
See number 2 above--most booksellers start filling out their spring, summer, and fall schedules right after the new year. Big-name bookstores will sometimes schedule signings months in advance, so be prepared to start early for those venues that are highly sought after.

4. The worst time for book tours: late November to early January
Winter is a tough time for signings at bookstores, but it can be a good time for presentations to clubs and professional organizations (although many organizations set their schedules early, so plan to start calling at the beginning of the year to obtain speaking spots).

5. The best time to hold giveaways for new books: just prior to or immediately after release, and ongoing
To help drive initial reviews and buzz, giveaways are best held just before a book is released or immediately after its release date. Some reader sites have specific windows for giveaways (Goodreads, for example, allows authors to give away prerelease copies of their books, but will only allow giveaways

for published books that are within six months of their release dates), so check the guidelines for timing. Ongoing giveaways are good as well, especially if you are an author with a number of books and can give away some titles to help drive sales of others.

6. The best time to book conference speaking engagements: six months to one year in advance

Those authors who would like to give presentations or workshops at conferences should plan to do so early--most conferences schedule presenters a year in advance, and some are even booking two years ahead. If you know you want to speak at a certain conference, check the website for dates when calls for presenters begin and note deadlines for submitting applications.

7. The best time to seek jacket blurbs: three to four months prior to publication

Most authors who are traditionally published will have help from their editors on soliciting blurbs for their back covers, but self-published authors have to do this work themselves. I recommend contacting those whose endorsement you seek at least four months prior to publication. Be considerate to those you're approaching and submit all or a portion of the book (this can be done in manuscript form) with enough time for the endorser to read what you've sent. And remember to acknowledge the generous gift of a positive blurb with a thank you afterward.

8. The best time to seek reviews: ongoing, but good to solicit some three to four months prior to publication, so that they are available when the book is released

Again, authors who are traditionally published will usually have help from their publishers with initial reviews, but self-published authors will have to handle reviews themselves. Traditional publishers will usually prepare Advance Review Copies (ARCs) and send them to top-tier reviewers (*New York Times*, *Publishers Weekly*, *Kirkus*, *Booklist*, *Library Journal*, etc.) four months prior to publication. Self-published authors can approach reviewers (generally, mid-tier and online) once their book is in printed form or, in the case of an ebook, when the formatted file is available.

9. The best days to pitch news producers and editors: Tuesday, Wednesday, and Thursday

When making publicity calls, I've found that the best days to actually reach news editors or producers fall during the middle of the week. Editors and producers tend to be busy or unavailable on Mondays, and Fridays seem to be the most difficult days to reach media people.

10. The best time of day to pitch radio and TV morning show producers: 6:00 to 8:00 a.m.

If you plan to pitch morning show producers, be ready to get up early. Most producers are in the studio well before 6:00 a.m. on days that shows are taped, and many of them will be unavailable once the show begins. If you miss a producer, be sure to leave a voice message and follow up with email information (press release, author photo, and book cover art). Be aware of time differences if you're calling across the country, too.

11. The best time to pitch media for event coverage: three weeks prior to event date

This is my own personal preference, but I like to give print media the most lead time for feature stories (about three to four weeks). If you are calling magazines, their lead times can be quite long--from three to six months in some cases--so research their submission guidelines and plan accordingly. I usually make calls to radio and television producers about two to three weeks prior to events (I like to set up my clients' events first, usually booking six months out, and then make media calls about three weeks prior to each event to help drive traffic to it).

12. The best time to send out calendar listings: two weeks to one month prior to event date

Many print and online publications will let you post listings on their websites. But check the guidelines for when listings must be done--most publications want them two to four weeks in advance of the event date.

Finally, many authors ask me about the best times to schedule their social media posts. For those who do a lot of posting on different sites, I suggest using a management dashboard like Hootsuite to schedule updates. As to specific timing, in his December 6, 2010, post on Problogger (http://www.problogger.net/archives/2010/12/06/wh

ens-the-best-time-to-publish-blog-posts/), Dan Zarella gives the following guidelines:

-The best day and time to post on Twitter: Friday at 4:00 p.m. EST is considered the most retweetable time of the week.

-The best time for readership on blogs: early morning.

-The best *days* for Facebook sharing: Saturday and Sunday.

-The best *time* for Facebook sharing: around 9:00 a.m.

CHAPTER 7. DISTRIBUTION

One of the most important elements for successful book publicity is having printed copies ready for distribution. While this may sound obvious to some, many authors ask publicists to promote their published work before the books are available for stores to order. This situation creates a dilemma for everyone involved: the bookseller, who wants to give the writer a signing date, but finds the book isn't available through the distribution channels he likes to work with; the publicist, who has to scramble to contact the publisher about the distribution issue; the publisher, who then has to contact distributors and buyers regarding the listing; and the author who misses out on a good signing event.

The few remaining chain bookstores in existence today, including Barnes & Noble, often prefer to order through their own distribution systems. This is an important concept for self-published authors to understand, because it can take a certain amount of time (sometimes up to three months) to get the books into the system. Publishers will handle applying for ISBNs and setting up distributors, but writers should be aware that doing so takes time. And not all publishers do their homework; I've worked with a few authors who've had their promotional efforts stalled while waiting for their book to become available to a certain distributor that a bookseller wants to use.

Many independent booksellers order through wholesale suppliers like Ingram Content Group or Baker & Taylor. And some bookstore managers are willing to order directly from the publisher, especially if the publisher allows returns and will give discounts or pay for shipping. But, due to high shipping costs and lack of shelf space for unsold copies, a growing number of booksellers are asking authors to bring books to signings. This is known as a "consignment arrangement," where the bookstore will take a certain percentage (usually 40 percent) of any books sold. So, in addition to the expense of purchasing the books themselves, authors also have to get them to the store, which can be a headache when the signing isn't local.

When I contact booksellers for book-signing dates, the first question they typically ask is not about the book's content or the author. They usually want to know the ISBN. Most of them will look up the book as we speak on the phone, and their second question is invariably whether the book is available for order. If they see a print-on-demand (POD) listing for the book, they often express concern about availability, so I urge my traditionally published clients to see if the publisher will consider printing an offset run of books that are available for orders. Most publishers, if there is enough demand for the book, are willing to do so.

The other concern for booksellers is returnability. If your publisher lists your book as non-returnable, most booksellers will pass on ordering copies for events. Some will allow consignment arrangements, but those who don't may not want to risk ordering books that they will be stuck with after your event is over, and will therefore pass on hosting you. For this reason, if you plan on appearing at bookstores and are using a small press to print your books, be sure to discuss listing your book as returnable before you begin your publicity campaign, so that you're not turned down by booksellers when you or your publicist begins making calls.

It can be tough out there for self-published authors who are marketing books for the first time. Not being ready to take book orders is a mistake that no authors want to make, especially when they often have one shot at a prestigious bookstore, speaking venue, or media appearance. Authors can assure themselves a much better chance at success if they take the time to get those proverbial distribution ducks all lined up before they kick off their promotional plans.

CHAPTER 8. CREATING YOUR PRESS RELEASE

I find in my discussions with new authors that many of them are unfamiliar with what a press release is or how it can best be used. So, listed below is a brief (okay, maybe it's not so brief!) overview of important considerations when writing and distributing releases.

A press release is a tool used by publicists to provide background information to media and other people interested in an author's work. If you don't have a publicist, you can write your own press release to use as background information, but because it has been such an important resource for the media community, expectations dictate that releases follow established public relations guidelines. In other words, if you are going to write a press release for your book, be sure to heed the following simple guidelines:

1. Think of your press release as a newspaper article. It should be written so that anyone you send it to can take it as is and publish it in a print publication or blog with minimal changes (and since most of the media are busy people, they will love you for making their job easier!). That means that it should be professional and succinct and should be written in a journalistic (i.e., focused on the who, what, when, where, and why of the story), third-person style.

2. Your press release should begin with the line, "For Immediate Release," which tells your media contacts that they are free to use the information that follows right away. Immediately following should be the date, written out in full, with the current year included (e.g., November 28, 2016).

3. Next is the headline, which should always be as succinct and intriguing as possible. Center your headline and be sure to include what's important, stating what is most exciting or unique in as few words as possible. Here's an example from a release about my book:

Publicist Paula Margulies Announces Second Edition Release of *Coyote Heart*, Native American Love Story Set in San Diego

4. The body of the press release should follow the headline. I like to use a five-paragraph structure for my press releases:

1) The introductory paragraph
Many PR professionals recommend starting with an intriguing lead-off or hook in the first paragraph of your release. Since I tend to make my initial pitches by phone, I usually forgo the hook and instead open with a journalistic introductory paragraph that gives the who, what, where, when and why of the release. The first paragraph should be prefaced with the city

and state where the event or content of the release is taking place. Here's an example of an introductory paragraph:

San Diego, CA–Book publicist Paula Margulies announces the second edition release of her debut novel, *Coyote Heart* (ISBN 978-0-9913545-0-4), a multicultural love story set against the backdrop of the Pala Indian Reservation in San Diego, California. The new edition can be found at Amazon.com, Barnes & Noble.com, and other outlets. Prior to the first edition publication, *Coyote Heart* received numerous awards, including an Editor's Choice Award at the San Diego State University Writers' Conference. *Coyote Heart* was also a finalist in the Santa Fe Writer's Project Literary Awards Program, a worldwide competition that included over 350 entries.

2) **An informational paragraph or two**
In the second and third paragraphs of the release, I like to give a succinct overview of general information about the subject of the release. This should be supplemental information to what you presented in the first paragraph. An example of two informational paragraphs follows:

Coyote Heart tells the story of Carolyn Weedman, a San Diego librarian trapped in a troubled marriage with a disabled husband. After a chance encounter with a widowed Pala Indian professor, Carolyn finds herself drawn into an unexpected love affair. Torn by conflicting feelings, she discovers a secret about her husband's past that forces her to confront her divided emotions and choose between the two men she loves.

Set against the backdrop of local politics on the Pala Indian Reservation, *Coyote Heart* explores the intricacies of illicit love and marriage, the strength that comes from sacrifice, and the courage to forgive the injuries of the past. The novel calls on several San Diego landscapes, including the Rancho Penasquitos preserve and the Pala Indian Reservation, to give the story a unique local flavor. Written with haunting natural imagery and lyrical prose, *Coyote Heart* tells a compelling tale of love and modern Native American culture.

If you have strong blurbs or testimonials you can also add a paragraph with that information:

The novel has received praise from established members of the writing community, including Pulitzer Prize-nominated journalist and former *Seattle Post-Intelligencer* editor Mark Trahant, and celebrated author Peter Rock, who writes, "With *Coyote Heart*, Paula Margulies uses lyrical, yet restrained prose to take us into a world where the usual definitions will not fit--where the personal and the political, even the human and the animal, become increasingly difficult to differentiate. This novel bravely explores the difference between a relationship that bends and one that breaks; it even suggests that a healed fracture is stronger than what was originally whole."

3) **Include a quote**
Since many in the media will, hopefully, use your press release verbatim, you'll want to include a quote in your release (so it looks as if you were interviewed by the publication running it). I like to keep quotes to one or two sentences. If you're writing about your book, a good topic for a quote is what inspired you to write the book. When quoting, always use tags in the past tense (i.e. "said Margulies," rather than "says Margulies"). Here is a sample press release quote:

"I wrote this novel, in part, because I've always been fascinated by what makes a marriage work," said Margulies. "My sense is that many marriages survive not because the two individuals involved are meant for each other, but because the losses and hardships that they've endured forge a bond that is difficult, and sometimes impossible, to sever."

4) **Include a brief bio**
The final paragraph of your release should include biographical information about you, but remember to keep it as succinct as possible. Summarize your history as a writer and include information about awards, other publications, media appearances, and any other information that positions you as an expert. I usually end the bio paragraph with a sentence about where the author resides or what the author is working on next, or both. Here's an example of a bio paragraph:

Paula Margulies is the owner of Paula Margulies Communications, a public relations firm for authors and artists. She has received numerous awards for her short stories and novels, and her essays have been published in a number of professional journals and magazines. She has been awarded artist residencies at Caldera, Red Cinder Artist Colony, Centrum, and the Vermont Studio Center. Margulies currently resides with her husband in San Diego, California.

You can also include a final line about where to find more information about you and your book:

For more information about the author or *Coyote Heart,* please visit www.amazon.com, or **www.paulamargulies.com**.

5) **End with contact information**
At the end of your release, be sure to tell the media contacts and their readers who they can contact for more information about you. You should include a line that reads, "For Further Information," and follow it with your (or your publicist's) name, address, telephone numbers, email and website information:

For further information, please contact:
Paula Margulies Communications
8145 Borzoi Way
San Diego, CA 92129
T: 858-538-2047
paulamar@san.rr.com
www.paulamargulies.com

If you are sending a release yourself, you may want to include your book's cover art in the upper left-hand corner as letterhead. Try to keep your release to one page; if you have to use a second page, be sure to label it as such with your last name and page number.

If your publicist has written the release, be sure to ask permission before changing its content and distributing it yourself (if it's written in your publicist's name, any changes must be approved by your publicist).

You will want to use your press release as a follow-up tool when pitching booksellers or the media. Send the release as an attachment, along with your headshot and book cover art (front cover only, in JPEG format) after you have made an inquiry for a signing event or media interview.

Once you have a general press release written, you can use it as the basis for announcing new events (media and book-signing appearances, awards, rereleases, etc.). You will need to change the release date, title, content paragraphs, and quote, and update your bio paragraph as information changes.

It's easy to distribute your releases on free press release distribution websites. My favorites are http://www.free-press-release.com and http://www.briefingwire.com. Some of the free sites require registration and many of them offer fee-based advanced exposure services. Some provide email tracking, showing the number of views your press release receives once it's on the wire.

Finally, if you have any questions about your release or feel uncertain about writing one yourself, consider asking a publicist or PR specialist to write one for you. Many PR professionals are willing to provide this service for you and should be willing to do so for a nominal fee.

One of the least expensive ways to promote your novel or nonfiction book is to create a Q&A (or an FAQ, if you prefer that title) and ask bloggers to post it on their blogs and websites. These postings can be coordinated to appear at certain times and dates (this is known as a blog tour), or you can approach individual bloggers and ask that they list your information in future posts.

Q&As are also useful tools to submit to radio and television producers and hosts before appearing in on-air interviews.

It's easy to create Q&As--use simple questions that all readers want to know about writers, and write brief, sincere responses to them. Examples of commonly asked questions include, "What was your inspiration for this novel/book?" "How long did it take you to write this book?" "Who are your favorite authors and why?" "What is your next novel/book about?"

Once you have a list you like, send it with a JPEG of the book cover art, an author photo, and other information about your book (ISBN, ordering information, links to websites, etc.). It's good protocol to follow the blogs where your information is posted and to include links to that blog or website on your own sites. Also, don't forget to thank those who agree to post information about you and your book after the post has run.

Here is a sample Q&A I've used in the past for the launch of the second edition of my first novel, *Coyote Heart*:

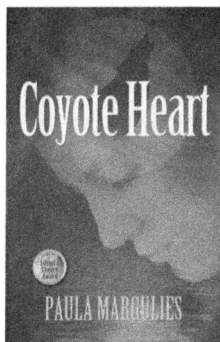

Coyote Heart, Second Edition

By Paula Margulies
ISBN: 9780991354504
Publisher: One People Press, January 8, 2014
$15.95
www.amazon.com
www.paulamargulies.com

Frequently Asked Questions

1. Where did you get the idea for this novel?

I had the idea for a short story about a married woman who falls in love with a Native American man. I don't know where this idea came from, but I kept seeing the image of the husband, who I imagined had been in an accident of some sort, sitting in a chair with a rifle in his hands and his arms raised up in a Native American victory gesture. This image haunted me so much that I began writing about it, and that evolved into the novel, *Coyote Heart*.

2. You're a hybrid author. Tell us how *Coyote Heart* **was originally published.**

I began *Coyote Heart* (then called *Bow and Arrow*) in 2003 and finished it in 2004. In January 2005, I took the manuscript to the SDSU Writer's Conference, where it won an Editor's Choice Award from Shaye Areheart, an editor at Crown Publishers. I met my agent, Bob Tabian, at the same conference, and in 2008, I was offered a royalty contract by a small press, which then published *Coyote Heart* in 2009. I regained the rights to it in 2013 and have now published it myself as a second edition.

3. In the story, the main character, Carolyn Weedman, who is married to an engineer, Everett, falls in love with Pala Indian professor Roy Washburn. Why did you want to tell a story about a woman who is unfaithful to her husband?

Initially, the story I envisioned was going to be about a husband and wife whose marriage falters, but then mends again. As I was developing the characters in this story, I realized that until something drastic happened–in this case, Carolyn having an affair with another man–there would most likely not be any reason to reconcile the differences that were breaking the marriage apart. I believe that the affair awakens feelings in both Carolyn and Everett; Carolyn has to choose between her new love and her marriage, and Everett has to face the fact that is wife might be leaving him. The affair forces both of them to come to terms with what is wrong in the marriage, and that, along with some other cataclysmic circumstances, leads them to the ultimate decision about whether or not they should stay together.

4. Carolyn's love interest, Roy Washburn, is a Pala Indian man who teaches British history at a local college. His son Luke, on the other hand, is a tribal activist. Why did you decide to give Roy a career that focuses on another culture?
In this story, I wanted to explore both sides of cultural heritage–those who embrace it and those who deny it. I decided Roy and his son would act as examples of two extremes in their views about their native history. With Roy, we have a character who has focused on another culture as a way of distancing himself from his upbringing, while Luke is someone who has embraced his cultural heritage to an extreme. Roy's focus on another culture is a source of pain for Luke, and vice versa–Luke's tribal identity borders on fanaticism, which drives a lot of the conflict in the story between the two men, especially when Carolyn, a white woman, comes into the picture.

5. The story, which is set on the Pala Indian Reservation in San Diego, has a subplot about a landfill issue there. Is the subplot based on true events and, if so, what's happening with them now?

Yes, the plan to place a landfill on sacred ground near Gregory Canyon is still an important issue on the Pala Reservation. There was legislation (SB 833) proposed in the California legislature to stop the project, and although the bill passed the legislature with only three opposing votes, Governor Brown vetoed it. In 2012, the Army Corps of Engineers issued a draft Environmental Impact Survey for public comment, and then held a public hearing in late January 2013 on the project. The response was great, with a number of proposed oral comments, so the Army Corps extended the written comment period of the draft survey. The project is still under investigation.

6. Do you have a favorite character?

I read somewhere that an author should love all the characters in her novel, and I feel that way about this one. The characters in *Coyote Heart* are all flawed and all have suffered some kind of loss, which makes me feel for each of them, but if I had to pick one, it would have to be Carolyn's husband, Everett Weedman. He is a rational man, who likes order and logic in his world yet, at the same time, he has a deep love of nature and he's willing to sacrifice for what matters.

7. Have you written any other books?
Yes, I recently published a collection of short stories called *Face Value: Collected Stories*.

8. What is your next novel about?
I'm working on an historical novel called *Favorite Daughter*, which is about Pocahontas, who tells the story in first person, in her own point of view. I recently read Sena Jeter Naslund's novel *Abundance*, which tells the story of Marie Antoinette in her own voice, and I was fascinated by the way it dispelled so many myths about her character, while showing us who she really was as a person. I'm trying to do the same thing in *Favorite Daughter*, by telling the story from Pocahontas's perspective and letting her show us the true nature of her relationship with John Smith and how she came to play such a significant role in American history.

CHAPTER 10. WHAT TO INCLUDE IN AN AUTHOR BIO

One of the most important pieces of an author's media kit is the biographical summary, or bio, which provides the important background information that media representatives, booksellers, conference attendees and, ultimately, readers seek. A good bio can be more than a means of introducing authors to their market; it also can provide a way to develop a platform for new authors who don't yet have a lot of experience or a public track record.

So, what kind of information should an author put in a bio, and how much of that information should be included?

I recommend that writers create two kinds of bios: a brief, one-paragraph summary that can be used in press releases and for program announcements or spots with limited space, and a longer piece that can be used for media promotion and speaking events.

The short summary I include in the press releases I write for my clients takes the form of a single biographical paragraph at the end of the release. This paragraph is factual in tone and generally includes the author's credentials, a summary list of other works and awards, a statement about where s/he currently resides, and what the author is working on next.

The longer, full-length bio I recommend is generally three to four paragraphs (I try to keep it to one page) and includes more detailed information about the author's personal history. This longer bio is the one I use when I approach the media to set up client interviews; it also can be submitted to conference or event organizers to help provide background for program listings and speaker introductions.

When writing a longer bio, I urge authors to include any information that might be of interest to a reporter or producer looking for topics for an article or a radio or television spot. Even if a writer doesn't have a celebrity background or prior experience publishing, the information provided in the bio can pique interest, especially if timed to tie in with current events in the news.

It's important to include any tidbits of information that might help a reporter or producer see a possible story for an article or interview. But since public relations is mainly a business of establishing relationships, a thorough and well-written bio can also help build a connection between the reader and the author.

Some potential items to build into a longer bio include the following:

1. The city and state where the author was born
2. Where the author went to high school
3. Where the author went to college or trade school and what major and degrees were pursued there
4. Significant achievements, including awards, titles, media coverage, or recognition
5. Experience or expertise in specific industries or arenas
6. A list of publications (including ongoing writing gigs), releases, exhibitions, patents, and creations
7. Tie-ins or connections to current events
8. Volunteer or altruistic work
9. Hobbies or special interests related to the content or subject area of the author's book
10. Relevant information on the author's family members
11. The city and state where the author currently resides
12. Future projects or a description of new projects the author is working on
13. Links to websites and blogs that provide more information about the author

Not all of this information will be relevant for all authors; writers should take a look at their subject areas and backgrounds and give some thought to what information might be most useful and interesting when promoting their particular books. If a writer has trouble deciding how much information to include, running a draft by a professional publicity or media person, or a trusted editor or writing partner, can help.

Generally, I recommend that the tone of the bio be professional and simple. Bios are typically written in third person, with the author's full name used the first time it appears, and only the last name used for each subsequent mention. If an author prefers a more informal tone and wants to use his or her first name for subsequent mentions, that's fine, as long this is done consistently. Some authors like to inject humor into their bios, but care should be taken to ensure that the piece is not too cheeky or off-putting and that the bio clearly provides the information that the reader seeks.

Finally, authors should remember that bios are living documents that need to be updated regularly as new events in the author's life (awards, publications, residential and job moves, personal developments, etc.) occur.

CHAPTER 11. YOUR AUTHOR PHOTO

It's important for authors to connect with their readers, and one of the best ways to do that is to include an appealing and professional author photo on your book covers and social media pages. A photograph gives your readers an idea of who you are and can help them identify you in future works.

Many authors try to cut costs by taking selfies of themselves and using those as photographs, but unfortunately, those photos often look homespun and unprofessional. In order to present yourself in the best light possible, you need to hire a professional photographer to take your author shot-- one who understands lighting, camera angles, backgrounds, and general photographic presentation to create a photograph that will resonate with your audience.

When hiring a professional photographer, it's a good idea to first take a look at the photographer's work and get a general idea of the style used when taking photographs. Once you've hired a photographer, be sure to ask what to wear to your photo shoot (the photographer may recommend bringing one or more outfits in different colors, in order to see what works best with the backgrounds for your shot).

I prefer studio (indoor) shots for author photos, but many authors opt for outdoor photographs of themselves. If you choose to go outdoors, take care that the background doesn't overwhelm the author in the picture. If outdoor shots are available, it's a good idea to ask your photographer to also take some indoor shots as well, in case the weather doesn't cooperate, or in case you decide you might like the indoor photo better.

It's fine for authors to include props (pets, books, pens, etc.) or additional garment items (hats, scarves, feather boas, etc.) in their shoots, but my recommendation is to try to make the atmosphere in the shot as professional as possible, while still presenting a friendly and approachable demeanor. Avoid sunglasses or any items that obscure your features and, if using props, be sure they don't dominate the photograph. And try to make your photograph more of a head shot (with an emphasis on your face, rather than a longer distance shot of your entire body), so that your facial features are clear in thumbnail-sized photos, like the ones you'll place on the back cover of your book.

Regarding whether it's best to use color or black and white photographs, I recommend color, but if you prefer to use black and white, that's fine. It's sometimes good to ask your photographer to shoot with both options, so that you can choose which format shows you in the best light.

It's also important to ask your photographer to provide you with JPEG files of your photographs in both high- and low-res versions. Since some photos erode over time online, it's nice to have them on a thumb drive or in a cloud server where you can access fresh copies of them as needed.

CHAPTER 12. REVIEWS AND CONTESTS

One of the most important early tasks for an author when promoting a book involves sending the book out to book reviewers at major newspaper, magazine, and publishing sites and entering it in contests.

The reason you want to do this early is twofold: so you have reviews and award recognition that you can share on the book's Amazon and other social media site listings when the book is released and, in the case of contests, to help boost the book's prestige and interest to readers and the media.

With regard to book reviews, there are two tiers of reviewers at magazines and newspapers: those referred to as top-tier, and others who are considered mid-tier. The difference between these two groups is that the top-tier reviewers (at publications like the *New York Times Book Review*, *Publishers Weekly*, *Kirkus Review*, *Library Journal*, etc.) typically review books published by traditional (large) presses. This group of reviewers may occasionally review books by self-published authors, but because of the overwhelming number of books released each year, most of them focus on those that are traditionally published.

These reviewers oftentimes require a long lead time to review a book before its release date (this window can sometimes be as long as four months). For this reason, traditional publishers will often issue an Advance Review Copy (or ARC) of the book in printed form, so that the top-tier reviewers and media who require longer time windows for reviews can read the book in the form it will take when it's released.

Many self-published authors who think they might want to take a chance on a review by these entities will need to prepare ARCs and allow for the longer lead times before releasing their books. Since preparing ARCs can be costly and top-tier submissions often force a longer wait to publish, many self-publishers choose to skip the top-tier reviews. For these same reasons, I suggest that self-published authors might want to start with the mid-tier reviewers. To do this, you'll need to have printed copies of the book available (many reviewers still request that books be submitted in printed form).

Some of my clients have asked if I will do these kinds of mailings for them, but I usually don't send out books to reviewers--authors should plan to handle that task, including packaging and postage, themselves (or ask if their publishers will do it), mainly because it can involve mailing a lot of books. Authors will need to order enough printed copies of their books to send to the reviewers they want to query, so it's a good idea to take a look at lists of media and print reviewers and plan accordingly.

Usually, submissions to book reviewers will also include a cover letter and a press release, along with one or two copies of the books; authors should always check with the reviewers' websites to see what they require in the way of book submissions.

With regard to contests, authors should peruse book contest sites (authors can find a list of contests on my blog at paulamargulies.blogspot.com) and consider which of them they want to enter. In most cases, entries will include a copy (or copies) of the book, along with an application form, and a check for the entrance fee. In some cases, contest organizers will ask that authors include a press release with their submissions.

Most contests list their submission requirements on their websites, so authors need to check those they're interested in to see what they require for submission (be sure to factor in a week or so when mailing physical book copies as part of submissions, so you can meet any deadlines listed on the contest sites). In many cases, the entries are organized by genre, and authors can oftentimes choose to submit books in more than one category. There are usually separate fees for each category submission, and since this process can become costly, authors will want to choose wisely when considering which contests and categories to submit to.

CHAPTER 13. BOOKING EVENTS LIKE A PRO

Many authors are leery of doing book tours, not only because it's expensive to travel across the country, but also because it's difficult to create a good-sized audience. How can a relatively unknown writer hope to guarantee crowds at signings? Here are some suggestions to help fill the seats, and hopefully, ring up sales:

1. **Sign in cities where you know people**
This sounds obvious, but I've had clients insist on appearing in cities like New York, Chicago, or Washington, D.C., when they don't know anyone there. Being an unknown makes setting up signings difficult in the first place, but if you go to a city where you don't know anyone, chances are you'll have a hard time filling the seats. Instead, consider places where you know people--the town where you grew up, the city where you worked at that start-up company that now owns half the block, the places your college roommates live, etc. Don't just think big city or target market demographics; instead, focus on places where you can call up half a dozen people and get them to each bring a friend to your signing (or at least post a notice at work in the company break room).

2. **Schedule your signings wisely**
During its heyday, Areopagitica Books owners Doug and Rebecca Rutledge in Columbus, Ohio, suggested holding a signing at one o'clock in the afternoon on Saturdays. Why was that a preferred

time? "Because," Doug said, "the farmer's market next door lets out then, and the overflow crowd tends to come into the bookstore to browse afterward." Likewise, James Jackson at the now-closed The Know Bookstore in Durham, North Carolina, used to recommend holding signings at seven o'clock on Friday evenings, right after the weekly jazz session that was held in the adjacent café. If you don't have a lot of fans, or aren't familiar with the city where you're signing, scheduling your reading right after a nearby or in-store event can help draw interested listeners in to hear you without costing you a dime in advertising.

3. **Think outside the bookstore box**

Many authors automatically want to hold readings at chain stores like Barnes & Noble, small independent book stores, libraries and, depending on the topic, schools and universities. But there are lots of other options for book-signing venues. If your book has a nonfiction topic or is specialty-based, you might consider finding related outlets for that topic or specialty. For example, if you've written a cookbook, you may be welcome at a local bakery or restaurant that features your style of cooking. If your novel has a romantic theme, you might consider speaking at a romance writers meeting or at one of the local singles get-togethers. Got a book with a political spin? There are numerous Democratic, Republican, and Green clubs looking for speakers on any number of topics. Written a civil war historical? Find one of the many reenactment clubs, and ask if you can speak at the next meeting.

Don't be afraid to look for enticing or rarely considered venues as possible outlets. Museums, concert halls, churches--any place where people gather is a potential venue for book signings. Camille Forbes, author of *Introducing Bert Williams: Burnt Cork, Broadway, and the Story of America's First Black Star*, once gave a reading at Woodlawn Cemetery in New York. "The cemetery signing was a great start to my book tour," she says. "The audience had a unique vested interest in Williams, since he's buried there." Not your typical venue, but people came, and she sold books.

Also, be sure to maximize your website as a place where interested readers can find ways to hear you speak (keep it updated!) or even "win" additional interaction with you. Contests are a great way to promote your book on the web and the possibilities are endless. You can run contests for phone interviews with book clubs, or even follow the lead of one enterprising writer, who offers a contest for filmmakers, allowing them to create entries using scenes from his novel.

4. **Hit the malls**
Although we don't see as many chain bookstores as we did in the past, we can still occasionally find bookstore outlets in malls and shopping centers. These stores can sometimes present good opportunities for author signings. Oftentimes,

managers won't have room for a signing inside their stores. But many of them are willing to set up authors at a table right outside the door, especially during the noon-time rush. "We get all kinds of business professionals at the mall during the lunch hour," one manager at the Los Angeles Mall once told me. And those professionals are interested in meeting authors and buying books. Melissa Wiles, who once managed the Borders Express Tower City in Cleveland, Ohio, described the same situation in her store. "I set up my authors outside in the mall walkway," Melissa said. "It's a great way for them to be seen." Melissa also would host an annual book-signing table during the holiday season. She invited seven or eight authors to come and sign during one of the busiest times of the year for book buyers.

Even though these mall bookshops are scarce these days, there may still be opportunities for exposure. If you find a bookstore where you'd like to appear, it's worth approaching the manager and working together to come up with creative options for a signing opportunity.

5. **Partner up**
If you don't have a lot of friends and family to call on, consider partnering with another writer for a joint signing. Perhaps you're a fiction writer with a story about a baseball-loving detective. That nonfiction writer you know with a book about coaching in the minor leagues might be just the person to partner with. You'll bring your friends and

acquaintances to the signing, and he'll bring his. And the book store manager will love you both for helping to sell two books at one event.

6. **Consider developing your own low-cost book tour**
I've heard about one writer who takes his annual vacation from his day job in the summer and uses those three or four weeks off to create his own book tour. He packs his wife and kids in the car (along with lots of copies of his book in the trunk) and schedules stops across the country with friends and relatives. At each town he visits, he prearranges bookstore signings and also gives talks at public schools, libraries, and universities. He stays with his friends and family, so he doesn't pay for high-priced hotels, and the folks he stays with help get the word out about his signings and talks.

7. **Promote on the cheap**
If your budget is thin, there are inexpensive ways to promote your signings. Create your own flyers and post them in super markets, college student centers, and community libraries. Email the same flyers to your friends and family and reward them (maybe with a complimentary copy of your book?) for passing the word along. List your signings in the event calendars on newspaper and magazine websites and on announcement sites like Craigslist. Mount printed posters of your book cover on foam core and send these to bookstores for in-store promotions. Give the owners at speaking venues your printed giveaways (bookmarks, postcards,

business cards, magnets, etc.) to hand out to customers and guests. And finally, if you're lucky enough to have a friend who's gifted at walking up to people and convincing them to come and hear you speak, ask that friend to work the room the next time you're scheduled to sign. You could even consider offering him or her a percentage of your sales. It might be the best money you ever spend.

CHAPTER 14. HOW TO MAKE THE MOST OF YOUR BOOK SIGNINGS AND EVENTS

For those of you getting ready to appear at bookstores for the first time, here are some helpful hints for making the most out of your signing experience:

1. If the bookstore is near you, stop by a week ahead of time and see what kind of promotion the staff is doing for your book. If they don't have any in-store promos going yet, offer to give them posters, bookmarks, magnets, etc., to put in a store window or to use to create a display.

2. Talk to your friends and family and try to get as many people as you can to attend your signing. Even if they've purchased the book before or attended other signings, ask them to come and help draw people in the store over to the area where you're reading. Send email announcements to everyone in your address book prior to signings and ask your workmates, students, clients, etc., to attend. Mention the signing everywhere you go--at work, in the grocery store, at the bank, etc. Make up simple announcement flyers and leave them everywhere you can (at the library, on bulletin boards, at coffee shops, and so on).

3. If you're bringing books with you, pre-sign a number of copies to help long lines move faster. After your signing, see if you can get the store to keep the presigned copies. You can make or order

stickers that say "Signed Copy" for the spine of the book--these will help the books move quickly on the shelves.

4. A few days prior to the signing, advertise your event on local websites that have calendar listings. Many local newspapers and weekly tabloids have event notice forms you can fill out online for free. Some have longer lead times, so start checking the websites early. You can also put a notice in the events section on Craigslist and on other free networking sites.

5. The morning of your signing, call and ask for the manager (if you're one of my clients, the names are on your signing schedule). Make sure the manager knows what time your signing will be held and has everything ready for you, including table, chairs, microphone, electrical outlet (if necessary), and so forth. Also, find out if your books are there; if they're not, bring at least twenty copies with you.

6. Get to your signing early and make sure tables and chairs are set up and your books are out. I've been to a number of signings where my clients have gotten there and nothing is ready, so be prepared for that. Be sure to place one of your promotional posters on the table with your books, so patrons passing by will see the cover art and, hopefully, stop to hear you speak.

7. Always have extra copies of your book with you, in case you have a big crowd. Bring plenty of pens

and don't forget to bring your business cards, so those who buy your books can get in touch with you later or find information on your website.

8. Be personable and friendly to everyone who walks by. Wait until there is a good crowd gathered before starting and, if there's no microphone, make sure you project your voice so those in the back can hear you (a good tip is to practice this at home in front of a mirror). Talk about what inspired you to write the book, what the story is about, what motivates the characters, and what you love about the book. Read a few pages, preferably something that has some action or conflict. Don't read too long--less is more with public speaking. Those in the audience will often have questions, so be sure to allow for some after you finish. And don't forget to chat with readers while you're signing--the more impressed the reader is with you and the book, the better chance that reader will tell others about it and help create the buzz you're looking for.

9. After the signing, thank the store manager and other staff who helped you set up. See if they'll stock any leftover copies and don't be shy about asking them to order more copies from your publisher.

10. Bring your digital camera or cell phone and have someone take pictures of you while you're signing. After the signing, post the photos on your website and blog and write about the experience, the readers you met there, the helpful staff, etc. Be

positive about the experience (even if it didn't meet your expectations) and encourage everyone to come out for your next signing.

CHAPTER 15. SCHEDULING MEDIA INTERVIEWS

An important aspect of any author's promotional plan is obtaining coverage in media and other outlets where readers might learn about the author and the work.

In order to obtain press coverage for a book, authors must remember that the media (and that can include radio, television, online articles and announcements, and articles that appear in printed publications) are interested in specific content.

The stories that appear in the general news media, for example, often feature local events or news that impacts the listeners or viewers for that particular media outlet. To be featured or interviewed on a radio or television program usually requires that the author and the book be somehow newsworthy, either in terms of real-time events that are happening or the general interests of its audience. This newsworthiness usually means that the book's content is tied to a recent event that is making news, or that it involves a story that will be considered news by the viewing or listening audience.

Likewise, Internet sites and print publications, including newspapers and magazines that feature stories on authors or books, are usually looking for content that is relevant to their specific audiences. Just as for the general news media, the story (the author or the book) must be somehow newsworthy or relevant to the readership of the online site or publication that is posting or publishing the story.

For this reason, I tell my clients that it's crucial to be familiar with the media we plan to approach, so we can understand what that outlet looks for when it posts news.

It's also important to have as many connections to the media outlet as possible, so that if we're approaching producers or editors, we have a compelling reason to contact them. In addition to the author's platform (which is often the first item that producers or editors will consider) and the book's content, it helps to have something else--an appearance at a local event, perhaps, or a prestigious award, or even a feature in another media outlet--to offer to persuade the media representatives that the story is worthy of being shared with their audiences.

Listed below are the general categories of outreach I do for clients with regard to media:

1. General Media Queries
Oftentimes I'm approached by clients who are not planning physical book tours or appearances, but whose platform or book content warrants general exposure to the press. In these cases, I like to focus on both local and major news outlets. The major news outlets generally include newspapers and magazine publications in major US cities (*New York Times*, *Boston Globe*, *Los Angeles Times*, *Chicago*

Tribune, etc.) and major television and radio outlets in those same areas. I also will approach the local news media in the author's home town, in which case the author is often the focus of the feature.

2. Media Queries Prior to an Author Event

For those authors who plan to go on tour or make appearances with their books, I generally recommend first booking the events (I like to book about six months worth of events from the time of a book's release) before contacting the media. Once the events are scheduled and confirmed, I then will approach the local media in the city for each appearance approximately two to three weeks prior to each event. At that time, I have the author, the book, and the event itself to pitch to producers and editors. Having an event scheduled nearby can often be a good hook for a radio, television, or print editor to include in the feature or interview. For this reason, I urge my clients to consider scheduling events, especially if they want media coverage in those cities.

3. Online and Print Article Submissions

Online and print articles can be powerful tools in an author's promotional toolbox. Most print magazines and newspapers will, in addition to the printed feature, also include the article in the publication's online site. Even for publications that exist only on online, the shelf life of these pieces can be long-lasting, because they are saved and stored and can usually be located by search engines for future generations of readers.

If clients want to pursue being featured in a magazine or newspaper, whether in print or online, I generally advise pitching a story or article idea as early as possible (typically three to four months prior to the date you'd like the publication to appear). Many publications post their editorial calendars online, so authors can see what topics the publications plan to cover and locate the deadlines for those submissions. If the author has hired a publicist, that publicist can handle those queries. If no publicist is available, the author will want to carefully research the publication and locate the appropriate producer, editor, or reporter for the topic being pitched. The next step would be to send a query, generally by email, outlining the topic and briefly explaining how the author's platform or book addresses the issue. When sending an email query, the author should be sure to attach a press release, a proposed outline if pitching a written piece, and any relevant photos.

Some authors are interested in writing articles about their processes or their books and would like to present these articles to publications for publishing. In these instances, I generally urge my clients to write two kinds of articles: a 500-word piece and a 2500-word piece, since these are the two preferred lengths for most online and print magazine articles. To come up with ideas for articles, my client and I will discuss the topics covered in the book and then choose one or two of them that are timely or might be of interest to a certain industry or publication audience. Once the articles are written, I will develop a list of possible publications and venues that might be interested and then query them. I usually include a press release, any relevant photos or artwork associated with the piece, and the article itself in Word format. These queries can take time to process--many editors have to submit ideas to a review board or an editorial group--so it may be awhile before we hear back on the submission.

In some cases, the publication will ask for exclusive rights to an article before publishing it. In those instances, you will have to decide if you want the piece to appear only in the publication requesting exclusivity, or if you'd prefer to offer it to other entities (in which case the publication wanting an exclusive will usually pass). There is no right or wrong answer to this decision--in some cases, if the publication is prestigious enough or reaches the right audience for an author's work, it might be worth offering exclusive rights to the piece. In other instances, authors can get more mileage from a piece if it is published in a number of targeted publications that don't require exclusive rights. As always, the decision is yours to make as the author of the article, so do what you feel is best for you in each instance.

CHAPTER 16. TIPS ON PREPARING FOR RADIO AND TELEVISION INTERVIEWS

Appearing on a radio or television show can be an important part of your book publicity efforts. But for some authors, especially those who spend the majority of their time in front of their computer screens writing, the thought of appearing on camera or speaking to a radio host live can be terrifying. To help you get ready for that infamous close-up, here are some tips for appearing in-studio for radio and television interviews:

1. Once you've booked an appearance at a radio or television station, find out who will be doing your interview. Make sure that the person interviewing you has a copy of your book in advance and, in addition to your press release and bio, a Q&A sheet with standard questions, so that the interviewer is prepared for your segment.

2. Give yourself plenty of time to get to the studio where your interview will be recorded or shot. Confirm directions and parking availability, and allow between one and two hours for the interview.

3. For television interviews, most media outlets recommend that your attire be business casual. If you're not given specific instructions by your publicist or media contact, plan to bring several options for the wardrobe department to consider. Try to avoid solid black, solid red, solid white, super-busy prints and shiny fabrics. Also, remember

69

that in some interviews, the viewers will only see you from the waist up, so, it may not matter what kind of shoes or trousers you wear. Usually there is a wardrobe person on set who can steam your clothes to ensure they are ready-for-camera. And there are often some additional wardrobe options available on set.

4. Women who are interviewed on television should also consider bringing a few jewelry options to go with the outfits they bring along. Smaller jewelry may be harder to see on camera, so bring necklaces and earrings of varying sizes. Men should plan to bring along extra ties with different color schemes (avoid busy or wild prints and shiny fabrics) to go with their shirts and jackets.

5. When you arrive on set, often your first stop will be make-up. If you have allergies to certain products or are wearing hard contact lenses, be sure to tell the person doing your make-up ahead of time (I once lost a contact lens when a make-up person got too ambitious with her eye shadow brush while prepping me for a commercial shoot!).

6. After make-up and wardrobe, you'll be escorted to the stage area of the studio, where you'll be seated in a chair and interviewed by a producer or news anchor. The interviewer may ask you questions ahead of time to get a sense of how you respond. Use any prep time you're given to ask questions you might have about speaking into the

microphone or where to focus your gaze during the interview.

7. When sitting in front of the camera, remember to sit up straight and try not to tilt your head when you talk. Also, be sure to look at whichever camera you're instructed to face, even if there are lights or other cameras off to the side. While the interviewer is asking questions, look directly at him or her, and don't forget to smile!

8. When answering questions during radio and television interviews, it's a good idea to rephrase the questions you're asked, so that they are somehow included in your answer. For example, if you're asked how long it took to write your book, you might answer, "It took me three years to write the first draft of *My Great Novel*," rather than simply, "Three years." Try to answer in complete sentences, and be sure to say the title of your book as often as possible.

Note: If you have issues with your voice, practice speaking into a recorder before doing radio interviews. Play back your recordings and notice where you may have raised or lowered your voice, or inserted too many "ums" and "ahs." Before television interviews, have someone film you on a video camera, or practice in front of a mirror. See if you're smiling enough, if you're keeping your eyes focused, and if your head is straight while you talk. And don't forget to practice using gestures with your hands to emphasize points (or tone it down if you move your hands too much).

9. Try to relax and forget that you are being recorded or are on-camera. Doing a radio or television interview is a great opportunity to introduce yourself and your book to potential readers. Be yourself and have fun!

10. When your interview is over, be sure to thank the producers, anchors, and staff members who helped you that day. Also, find out when your segment will air and if there are clips or podcast links available of your interview. Let everyone on your email lists and social networking sites know when your spot is airing, and don't forget to post any clips or audio recordings of your interview on your website or Internet fan page.

CHAPTER 17. THE BLOG TOUR

When promoting a book, it's important to explore as many different methods as possible for getting it in front of readers. In-person signing events and presentations can help spread word-of-mouth with audiences face-to-face, and radio and television interviews can help reach those readers who watch and listen to media programs. But one of the most effective ways to reach readers is via the Internet. For this reason, I recommend that authors consider doing a blog tour to help get important exposure to readers online. There are hundreds of book bloggers (individuals who write about and review books on the Internet) and many of them have high numbers of followers who actively read their posts. A well-placed post on a highly regarded blogger's site can be a wonderful way to gain visibility for a book.

But there's a catch: although they can be quite effective as a promotional tool, blog tours can be a time-consuming proposition for authors to organize on their own. There are many steps involved in locating and querying bloggers to request a post on their sites. And there are no guarantees that the bloggers, who are often overwhelmed with author requests, will say yes.

The first step in organizing a tour is to identify bloggers on the Internet who cover books in your genre. This step requires that you comb the Internet for blogs that promote books similar to yours and then, once you've found them, locate contact information for reaching the blogger (I usually look for the blogger's name and email address; some bloggers will provide online contact forms in lieu of a direct email address).

Once you've developed a list of bloggers and have established contact information, the next step is to check the blog to see if the bloggers are currently accepting submissions. Most book bloggers do so on their own time, with no compensation, and many of them are overwhelmed with requests, or have decided to put their sites on hiatus. You don't want to waste your time contacting bloggers who aren't accepting submissions, and you also don't want to risk angering them by sending information when they've posted on their sites that they don't want to be contacted with queries.

After you've established a list of bloggers accepting submissions and have the proper contact information for reaching them, the next step is to query them to see if they'll be willing to host your book on a scheduled date. The hosting can involve posting an author interview, posting a book review (which can take some time, since the blogger has to read the book first before creating the review), and/or hosting a giveaway on their site for one or more of your books.

When you query a blogger, you'll want to send a brief email message outlining who you are, what your book is about, and what you're looking for in the way of a post (Q&A interview, book review, giveaway, or any combination of these options). You'll also want to let them know if the giveaways will be print or ebook copies (or both) and how many of those you're willing to supply.

Most important for the query is to include a press release, a Q&A (many bloggers will use the Q&A as their interview, so this is an important piece to include), and JPEGs of the book cover and your author headshot. These should be included as attachments. Please note that it is essential that the press release and Q&A be in Word format (not PDF), so that the bloggers can cut and paste from them as they choose.

Many bloggers will want you to offer print copies as giveaways; if you reside in the United States, you will want to offer print copies to readers in the United States and Canada only, to save on postage costs. Some bloggers may also want ebook giveaways for those outside of the United States. They usually run the giveaways using embedded giveaway platforms like Rafflecopter and will notify you (with the name and address) when they have a winner. Note: the majority of ebook winners will want their copies in either MOBI or standard ebook formats, so be sure to have those versions available before you offer ebooks as giveaways.

When I set up blog tours for authors, I usually send queries in batches of twenty to thirty. From each batch, we usually get about two to three yes responses (so, for two hundred queries, you're looking at a total of about twenty blog appearances).

Most bloggers will post the Q&A you send them, but some may want to provide their own interview questions for you to answer. Many will offer to review the book, and those who do usually will post the reviews on Goodreads and Amazon, as well as on their blogs. They'll ask what dates you want them to post, so a good rule of thumb is to spread your post dates out over a few months, so you have ongoing live exposure (some will need that lead time to review the book).

Once a blogger has posted an interview or review of your book, you'll want to share the link to the post on your social media sites. It's also crucial to thank the blogger (I recommend that authors do this online in the comments section of the post) for hosting you. There are a number of reasons for not skipping this step, the most important being that if you plan to write another book, you may want to approach the blogger again, and a sincere thank you will go a long way to helping him or her remember you the next time around.

If all of this sounds a bit daunting (or time-consuming), trust me, it is. For this reason, authors will usually hire blog tour agencies or publicists to set up and handle their blog tours. Doing so can be a good idea, because most of us who set up blog tours have developed relationships with bloggers and often have a stable of them who are willing to post for us. For example, I have lists of over a thousand mystery, romance, feminist, YA, sci-fi/fantasy, and general fiction bloggers. I also have nonfiction lists for books in specialty areas like general business, leadership, technology, cooking, parenting, and more. These are lists I've developed over years of handling blog tours for authors, and many of the bloggers on my lists have come through for me time and again.

But I spend a lot of time on the lists, updating them with new bloggers and deleting those who no longer seek author submissions, or who have suspended their sites. I have also developed relationships with each blogger, so that they know when I send in queries, the book is a good match for their blog style and followers.

One of the nice aspects of the blog appearances is that they may live forever online. In addition to sharing post links on your social media sites, you can also list them on your website. That way they will always be there for those who may come along later and want to see what the bloggers have said in the past about your book.

Finally, it's important to remember that the bloggers who host authors do so out of the goodness of their hearts. They love books and love to read, and the fact that they're willing to share information about authors and their work makes them the unsung heroes of the book marketing industry. Be respectful and grateful to them, and you will develop some significant advocates who will help to get the word out about your books.

CHAPTER 18. USING SOCIAL MEDIA

Many of my clients are stumped by the social media aspect of marketing their books. They understand that establishing a strong social media presence is important, but a good number of them avoid it because it appears time-consuming and somewhat daunting.

But creating an effective social media marketing strategy doesn't have to be difficult. I recommend that authors focus on sites that will give them the most bang for their time and effort. Rather than attempting to establish a presence on all sites, it's better to start with two or three of them. For those new to social media, I usually recommend beginning with Facebook, Twitter, and Goodreads, and building a presence on those sites first before expanding to others.

As far as what to post on a site, the most important concept to understand is why readers use social media in the first place. Most people don't visit social media sites in order to be sold goods and services; they're there to connect with others and to learn about topics that interest them. So, the best way an author can sell books via social media is to build relationships with readers. Authors will find the most success by being themselves and sharing items that are relevant to them personally. And those interested in the same topics are the best folks to friend or follow; ultimately, they'll be likely to follow back and peruse an author's posts and tweets with interest.

Here are ten tips on how authors can make their social media sites work for them:

1. Start your social media efforts early, at least a few months before your book is scheduled for release. Many authors wait until their books are out before becoming active on or participating in social media sites. Don't wait until the last minute--it takes time to build an audience, so give yourself a few months to friend or follow others and develop relationships. And don't stop with a few friends or followers; set aside time each week (one hour a week is plenty) to follow others and add friends to each of your social media sites.

2. Use your author name as your Twitter handle and your Facebook page title. Take some time and prepare a good, strong sentence for your bio (my recommendation is to keep it professional and brief, and avoid overused catch phrases regarding food, cats, being a nerd, and so on.). Also, for consistency, be sure to use this same biographical sentence on all your social media sites. Include a photo of yourself rather than your book cover; this helps with the relationship-building, so that readers identify with you as a person. Include a link to your blog or your website, so that readers know where to go to find out more information about you.

3. Focus on readers (as well as thought leaders and other writers in your genre) in your posts and tweets. Spend some time determining who your target reading audience is, where you can best reach those readers, and what will interest them the most.

4. Be a generous participant--post often on your social media sites. Share information that you find interesting or that you think readers might like.

5. If you're stumped on what to post, retweet others' posts on Twitter, and express your thanks when others retweet you. Comment on readers' blogs and social media sites and link back to posts that you find interesting or that you think your readers might like.

6. Use dashboards like Hootsuite, Threadsy, or TweetDeck to schedule posts on social media sites. Be sure to schedule at different times to reach readers who reside in different time zones. If finding time to manage your sites is an issue, consider hiring someone to do some of the scheduling work for you. It doesn't have to be expensive; a tech-savvy high-school or college student can be a great help with scheduling posts and updating information on sites.

7. Don't be a selfish friend or follower--refrain from posting constant invitations to buy your book, and be judicious about sharing snippets from your work. Instead, be a source of information for your followers; build relationships with them by

providing valuable information and responding to their questions and comments in a friendly, professional manner.

8. Use your social media sites to distribute interesting information about yourself or your book. Announce contest wins, event appearances, new releases, blog posts, and general news that will help readers learn more about you and your book. Do this without pressuring your audience to buy; instead, keep the focus on providing information and developing relationships with your readers.

9. Offer to guest post on other bloggers' social media sites and blogs and return the favor to those who might be interested in appearing on your sites. Contact other authors whose work is similar to yours or who write in the same genre, and consider working together to create genre- or topic-specific blog sites with posts you can then share with your social media followers.

10. Finally, be careful with the content on your social media sites. Steer clear of political or religious statements, and avoid undue criticism of others. Your goal is to build relationships, not destroy them, so avoid any topic that is likely to offend readers who might not share the same views.

CHAPTER 19. WHY YOU MIGHT WANT TO RETHINK YOUR TWITTER BIO

Many social networking pundits agree that Twitter can be a powerful tool for authors looking to sell their work. Media expert Jonathan Gunson, for example, calls it the most effective book advertising tool ever.

But like most social media tools, Twitter is only powerful if you use it effectively. If you're an author hoping to use Twitter to sell books, then how you describe yourself on Twitter is an important component to getting a potential reader to follow you. It can also help a book blogger, reviewer, or media producer/editor who is researching you learn more about how you've positioned yourself as an author. Remember, how you describe yourself on social media sites is a crucial part of creating a platform and presenting yourself to those who might buy your books.

With that in mind, here are my thoughts (from a publicist's perspective) on the do's and don'ts for authors regarding how they describe themselves on Twitter and other social networking sites. First, the don'ts:

1. **Don't deprecate yourself**
I'm stunned at the number of authors out there who describe themselves in unappealing terms. Some of the most common self-deprecating monikers are "loser," "geek," "nerd," "newbie," and "wannabe."

I recently came across one author who described her own books as "smutty," another who claims that he is an "ineffective woman chaser," a third who calls herself a "troll." Now I know that some of these descriptions are written to be funny, but there is so much overuse of these kinds of statements that they've lost their uniqueness and risk falling flat with readers. Some might argue that the terms "geek" and "nerd" are a badge of honor for those who consider themselves technically competent, but if that's true, consider positioning yourself with more positive words that might entice readers, bloggers, reviewers, and media folks to see you as an expert, rather than a person who describes him- or herself with overused and self-deprecating terminology.

2. **Don't label yourself as "aspiring"**
Okay, maybe you're new at the writing game, but if you're in the process of writing anything, even for the first time, it's perfectly okay to simply refer to yourself as a writer (no "aspiring" adjective necessary).

3. **Don't say you're a best-selling author unless you truly are**
There are best-selling authors out there, most of whom either have big-time breakout successes or extensive backlists. In either case, these people have sold many, many books. If that isn't true in your case, please don't label yourself as something that you aren't.

4. Use religion and politics as descriptors only if relevant to your readers

Many authors list Jesus as the first item in their Twitter bios. Others throw in the terms "conservative" or "liberal." While this kind of disclosure is fine for those who write Christian or political books, it's not always great for selling. Remember, some of the readers you may be looking to attract will not be Christian (or Buddhist, or Jewish, or whatever other religion you've mentioned). Likewise, if you list yourself as liberal or conservative, you're sure to scare off the other half of your potential readership. Keep religion and politics out of your descriptions, unless you want to sell only to those who think, and believe, as you do.

5. Don't refer to your husband, wife, or kids in your bio, unless they have something to do with your book

Listen, we're all members of some family or another. Unless your book is about parenting or family relationships, consider saying something else about yourself that potential readers might find more interesting and relevant.

6. Easy on the cat references

The other extremely overused descriptors I see out there are "cat-lover," "cat-owner," "owner of [x number of] cats," and the like. Unless you've written a book that has something to do with felines, consider leaving Fluffy where Fluffy belongs, on your living room couch.

7. Food is good, but watch that it doesn't become the only thing that sets you apart

If you're a cookbook author, then yes, by all means mention certain types of food in your handle. But if you're not, realize that mentioning anything having to do with coffee (or caffeine), alcohol, or chocolate has been used by thousands of other Tweeps who can't find something more creative to say about themselves.

8. Don't overkill with hashtags and website addresses

#There's #nothing #worse #than #trying #to #read #a #string #of #words #that #are #preceded #by #hashtags #or #anything.com.

9. Don't say "I follow back"--just do so

Enough said.

Now for the do's:

1. Think like a journalist

The best advice for positioning yourself to your readers comes from the school of journalism, where writers are advised to focus on the who, what, where, when, and why of the story. The same guidelines apply for your Twitter bio: tell potential followers who you are, what genre you write, and, if relevant, name your books. A good example is the bio for well-known mystery author L. J. Sellers, who has described herself thus: *Author of the bestselling Detective Jackson mysteries &*

standalone thrillers: The Sex Club, The Gauntlet Assassin, The Baby Thief, and The Suicide Effect

2. Keep your bios brief

No one likes overkill in anything, even Twitter bios. Remember that less is more when it comes to describing yourself, so be brief and descriptive. A good example comes from self-publishing guru J. A. Konrath, whose Twitter bio is simple and elegant; at one time it was simply, *I write thrillers.*

3. Keep them on point

If your goal is to use Twitter to sell books, then make sure that's a main point of reference when you describe yourself. If you have other goals for yourself, list them in your bio. For example, best-selling suspense author Bob Mayer has described himself thusly: *NY Times Bestselling Author, Speaker, Consultant, Former Green Beret, CEO Cool Gus Publishing*

4. Be professional

In summary, if you want yourself and your books to be taken seriously by readers, then be serious about how you present yourself on social media sites. Your potential Twitter followers (and, hopefully, future fans) will thank you for it.

CHAPTER 20. CONVENTIONS AND TRADE SHOWS

For those authors looking for speaking opportunities, there are other options besides bookstore signings and library appearances. One of those I urge my clients to consider, especially those who have a platform that allows them to appear as an expert on a topic, is to speak at conventions and trade shows.

Authors who have written nonfiction books on a particular subject area are best suited for this, especially if the content area has a large professional following. There are often trade groups and professional organizations that put on annual conferences and events for their members, and speaking at one of these events, especially if it is a large one, can bring good exposure to authors. Many conventions and trade shows will also host book sales for their speakers, so the events provide opportunities for you to sell books and gain exposure as an author/expert during a presentation.

Those authors who have written books on writing or publishing may want to try to appear at writers' conferences and book fairs. There are many scheduled every year throughout the United States and around the world, and most of them include opportunities for speaking on a wide range of writing topics.

But what about fiction authors? Are there convention and trade show opportunities for them?

The answer is yes. A novel or short story collection often contains themes or elements that can be discussed with professional organizations interested in those subjects, and many of them have local groups or chapters. For example, romance authors can find speaking opportunities at the many Romance Writers of America (RWA) groups, while crime and mystery authors can find opportunities at organizational gatherings put on by Sisters in Crime, Bouchercon, Left Coast Crime, Men of Mystery, and ThrillerFest.

Authors of science fiction and fantasy can find opportunities at the many sci-fi conventions that occur each year (Comic-Con, Worldcon, Dragon Con, etc.). Likewise, there are conventions for fan fiction and for poetry.

The key to appearing as a speaker at a conference or trade show is to be prepared. Authors who would like to present at a conference should consider the following :

1. **Research the organization and event and be sure you offer something that will interest attendees.**
There are lots of conferences out there, but not all of them may be a fit with your background or your book's content area. If you're not already familiar with the organizations you plan to approach, research them by visiting their websites, talking to their members, and reaching out to their conference organizers.

2. **Plan ahead**.
Many conference organizers book speakers one to two years out, so timing is important when contacting potential speaking venues. In many cases, authors will find that as soon as an annual conference or trade show is finished, planning for the next one begins. In some cases, speakers may be booked out two years in advance. Again, it's wise to take time to research those organizations to which you might be interested in speaking by visiting their websites often and checking the deadlines for queries or calls for submissions.

3. **Prepare two to three presentation descriptions to submit when querying conference organizers**.
Once you decide that there is a conference or trade show where you would be a good fit as a speaker, you'll have to query the conference organizers and submit a proposal for the presentation you want to give. I recommend to my clients that they prepare one or more presentation descriptions; sometimes it's good to give organizers options for your talk. Create a title for each presentation and write a brief, one-paragraph overview of what the presentation will cover and what attendees will learn from hearing your talk. I also recommend including a brief, one-paragraph bio with the presentation description that conference organizers can use in their programs if you're selected to speak.

4. Decide if you need audiovisual equipment or display items for your presentation, so you can let conference organizers know what you need ahead of time.

Many conference venues offer projectors and screens for presentations, but it's always a good idea to check with the event organizers in case they don't. In many instances, you may have to supply some or all of the equipment you need, so be prepared if that happens. It's also a good idea to have your PowerPoint slides, or any other media items you'll be using, available in a number of formats (on your laptop, on a flash drive, emailed to the event staff or yourself, in printed format, etc.) in case equipment isn't compatible or other issues arise with the venue's audiovisual setup.

5. Prepare to travel and, in most cases, cover those costs yourself.

Many authors assume that conferences and trade shows will pay for travel and hotel and offer a stipend or honorarium, but oftentimes this isn't the case. If the organization is offering to cover travel or provide a stipend, the specific details of what they're willing to cover are presented right up front, when your presentation submission is accepted. Sometimes costs are negotiable; for example, you might not have travel or hotel covered, but the organization may be willing to provide lunch or dinner for you after your talk, or may offer money to cover gas costs if you're driving. Always be respectful of the organization's decisions in this regard; many of them, especially if they're small, do not have the funds to cover speakers for their events.

In most cases, expect that there will be no compensation for speaking or travel, which means you'll have to decide if the exposure and potential book sales that occur as a result of appearing at an event are worth the cost of getting there. In some cases, appearances can provide networking opportunities, or chances to meet key people in the field, or they may lead to future speaking opportunities with other organizational representatives who might be in attendance. For these reasons, I always urge authors to take a chance and make as many convention and trade show appearances as they can afford.

6. **Allow time for decision-making on conference and trade show queries**.
Many conferences are organized by committees and those committees need time to review submissions and choose those speakers who will best fit their programs that year. In some instances, it can take months for committees to meet and make decisions; in those cases, it's best to be diligent in following up with the organizers, so that you are aware of when decisions will be made.

Once you've been selected to speak at a conference or trade show, be sure to schedule time for travel to and from the event. Allow for shipping of books or other items, and scheduling of promotional advertising and media appearances. It's also a good idea to have back-up plans if, for example, the audiovisual equipment fails or is not compatible with your laptop or other devices. When I speak at conventions, I always prepare hard copies of my PowerPoint slides in advance. They come in handy as handouts, but they can also be lifesavers if the audiovisual equipment for some reason doesn't work (I've had this happen twice at different venues where I was presenting).

In addition, be sure to bring promotional material, including standing posters, handouts, bookmarks, and business cards, to have on the table when you're presenting and to use afterward to promote your books, website, etc., to conference attendees.

Finally, don't forget to send a thank you to the conference organizers and staff who helped make your appearance a success. Doing so will help cement their impression of you as a professional and aid them in remembering you next time you approach them for a speaking opportunity.

CHAPTER 21. BOOK TRAILERS: DO YOU NEED ONE?

In a recent Random House/Zogby poll, 46 percent of respondents indicated that they spent the same amount of time reading as they had in the past year; 23 percent are spending more time reading (a good thing), while 30 percent said they are reading less than usual.

It's this last group that we all need to think about. The trend these days, especially for the younger set, is that people are reading less than in previous years.

So, what are these 30 percent who read less doing instead? Nearly two-thirds of them (65 percent) told Zogby that they're spending more time online, while 37 percent spend more time watching television or movies and 18 percent claim to be devoting more time to computer and video games.

These results show why so many writers are now making book trailers (a term coined by Circle of Seven Productions CEO Sheila Clover) to promote their work. For those who haven't seen one, a book trailer is basically a one- to three-minute promotional video about the book. The majority of them are mini-documentaries that include voice-overs, visual images, and some type of musical score. A few have actors portraying scenes from the book, and some include author sound bites or even (least recommended) authors reading their work.

Most authors run these on their websites and social networking sites like YouTube and Facebook. And publishers run them, as well. In fact, according to a recent *Wall Street Journal* article, many publishers are now creating divisions dedicated to making book trailers for their authors.

With so many readers spending time on the Internet, it makes sense for authors to use the web as a promotional space for their work. Yet many authors make the mistake of creating videos and plunking them down on their websites, assuming that just having them there will entice readers to buy their books. It's true, having a book trailer out there is important. But even more important is working it. Like your business card and press release, a video does no good unless someone sees it. That means you need to tell everyone you know, including the media, about it and invent creative ways to distribute it.

And that's where a good publicist comes in. Your publicist can announce your book trailer release to the media, send out copies to reviewers and booksellers (in the old days, we sent video news releases--VNRs--on VHS tapes; now we send links to your trailer), and use your video to market to distributors, bookstores, universities, and libraries. It's all in the pitch, of course, but having a good video and a sharp publicity person working for you can help get your book the attention it deserves.

CHAPTER 22. PRICING AND BOOK SALES

You will have two different prices for your book--one for the print version, and one for the ebook version.

The print version of the book will have a bar code label on the back cover with the book's thirteen-digit ISBN and a second, standard five-digit pricing code of "90000," which stands for "no price given." If you want that five-digit code to have the price of your book, you can put it there, but I would go with the standard code (if you bought your ISBN or bar code label or both from Bowker, it will have the standard pricing code on it).

You are also free to list a printed price somewhere on the back cover of the book; if you choose to do so, I recommend going with $15.95 (this is the price I recommend for listing on CreateSpace, too). This price is considered the ceiling for paperbacks by many bookstores. Any higher, and stores have trouble selling it. If the book is small (fewer than 200 pages), I recommend a price of around $12.95, but otherwise, $15.95 will probably be a good price to start with for the print version. Amazon will discount the print version price a certain amount on its site (this is to compete with used copies of the book that others will sell online).

Many self-published authors ask whether they should produce hardback versions of their books. While that decision is up to them, I generally recommend that they consider skipping the hardcover step and issue their books in ebook and paperback formats, since these are typically the most affordable options for most readers.

For the ebook, I recommend a price of $2.99. This is the lowest amount you can use and still receive the 70-percent royalty from Amazon. If you drop the price below $2.99, the royalty rate drops to 30 percent. My uploading consultant recommends listing the ebook version at $0.99 initially, when you first place it online, to help give it an initial sales push. I usually leave my books at $0.99 for two weeks when I first place them on Amazon, and then change the price to $2.99. If your ebook is $0.99 or free, there are a number of websites that do ebook promotions and announcements (some for free and some for a fee) where you can list the $0.99 or free sale of your book.

As time goes on and sales slow, your book's rankings will drop (this is normal for many ebooks---don't panic when it happens). When the rankings drop below 1 millionth, I usually recommend putting the ebook back on sale at $0.99 (or make it free if you have other books to sell), so that you can list it again with the promotional websites and get some copies sold. The new sales will push it back up in the rankings and then, after a couple of weeks, you can move the price back up to $2.99. We call this "pulsing" the price--the sales are a way to generate interest in the book and give you something to announce on your social media sites.

CHAPTER 23. EMAIL LISTS AND NEWSLETTERS

Although not a direct part of publicity per se, authors may want to consider using email lists and newsletters as a way of reaching readers who are followers of their work.

Email Lists
Building an email list can be a great way for new or experienced authors to build a following and get their message heard. Email lists allow authors to contact and engage with their readers on a personal level in a manner that is both direct and cost-effective. The key is to continually develop the email list over time, so that it becomes a working online marketing tool.

Developing an email list is not difficult. Authors can add a simple "Receive Notifications by Email" button on their websites, social media sites, and blogs to encourage visitors to sign up for future announcements. It's also a good idea to include sign-up sheets at in-person events, so that attendees who have heard you speak can join your newsletter roster if they choose.

Authors can also include colleagues, associates, friends and relatives, as well as readers and other authors they meet while networking at events such as writing festivals, book signings, and conferences, and those they connect with online.

Another way to encourage readers to join your email list is to put a call to action at the end of both the print and ebook copies of your book. That way, readers who enjoyed your work can sign up to stay current with news about you and your future works. Likewise, if you offer a newsletter for readers, you can remind subscribers to share the newsletter information, with a call to action included for those who receive shared copies.

Authors may want to include an email signup link in their bios, especially when guest blogging. Another way to remind readers to join is to include a link in their email signature block.

As far as how to use the list, you'll want to be sure to send out an email message every time you have news to announce. These announcements can include informing your readers and fans about a new book launch, a contest win, or the publication of a new edition of the book. Take care not to inundate readers and fans with too much news-- constant email messages can, over time, become intrusive and off-putting to your subscribers. Be judicious and respectful in your communications and share only items that are newsworthy or of interest to your subscribers.

Newsletters
Newsletters can be an extremely effective way for authors to stay in touch directly with readers and fans. Of course, they take time to write and format, so authors deciding to use this method of promotion

should have a fairly large list of recipients ready before they take the plunge.

The challenge for authors who choose to create newsletters for their fans is how to make the newsletter relevant and interesting. Here are some tips for creating newsletters that your readers will look forward to receiving:

1. **Keep it brief**
Since most readers have little time these days for promotional messages, it's best to keep your newsletter articles as simple and brief as possible. Aim to share information that's really news and, most importantly, that will resonate with and interest your readers.

2. **Make it about the reader**
When designing each issue of your newsletter, be sure to ask yourself, "What is it that my readers will want to read?" Keeping the newsletter focused on the reader, rather than on you, will help recipients look forward to receiving your newsletter (and will hopefully keep them from deleting your messages when they appear in their email in-boxes).

3. **Share only original content**
To help make your newsletter more relevant to readers, consider offering items of interest that you've not covered elsewhere (in a blog post or guest post, for example). Share fresh industry news, tips on writing, or updates about you and your

books, but try to not duplicate information that readers may have seen from you elsewhere.

4. Include information about appearances and events

Be sure to update your readers on upcoming appearances and events, so that those who haven't had the chance to meet you can do so, if they choose. Also, having a list of appearances to share with readers lets them know that you are serious about promoting your book, and that you'd like the opportunity to meet them.

5. Announce book launches and releases well ahead of time

One of the important advantages of having an author newsletter is that you can let your readers and fans know about new releases. Be sure to let your readers know about your progress with books you're currently writing and when you expect those books to appear. If there are preorder options for new releases, be sure to share information on how to obtain those books. Also consider offering sneak peeks, discounts, and other promotional options to your newsletter readers first, before making them available to others; this will help your newsletter continue to be valuable to your fans.

6. Make it personal

Since your newsletter is for fans and readers who are familiar with your work, be sure to share information with them in a way that shows that you appreciate them. Discuss items in your books (characters, settings, themes, research, for instance) in a way that is personal and open, and you'll have newsletter readers looking forward to future issues.

CHAPTER 24. WHAT TO INCLUDE IN YOUR WEBSITE

A good website is an important promotional tool that authors shouldn't ignore. I tell my clients that having a good website is like having a landing spot for their books--in addition to being a place for readers to learn more about authors and their books, author websites are also a place where authors can establish and grow their online platforms.

Not only does your website present a way for a publicist to gauge an author's readiness for representation, but media folks, reviewers, booksellers, and venue hosts will also visit your author site, so having a good website is a must if you are wishing to pursue book publicity.

Many of the authors who contact me are not certain about what they want their websites to accomplish. In order to have a good website, it's important to first know why you're building one. What is the primary goal for your site? Is it to sell books? Build your platform? Create a community for readers? Build followers on your social media sites? Once you've determined the site's primary purpose, it will be easier for you to know what to include in terms of content and design.

Once you have established a goal for your site, you need to consider content and design. Listed below are the components I feel are important to consider when creating an author website:

1. **A clear and compelling design**

Author websites don't have to be complicated or expensive, but they do need to be easy to navigate and appealing to viewers. It's best to have a professional company design your site, but a number of inexpensive options exist for website development, so choose a design platform that fits your budget.

When designing your site, think about the many ways that readers view them--on desktop monitors, laptops, tablets, and cell phones. Your website design should be easy to see in all of these viewing modes, so design accordingly. Also, remember that the more graphic content you build into the site, including things like videos and animation, the more time the site may take to upload. In general, opt for simple, clean concepts that allow readers to access information easily and quickly.

I usually advise clients who plan to write more than one book to develop an author website, rather than creating multiple individual book sites. Doing so allows authors to add new books as they become available, rather than having to create a separate website for each book.

2. **A good landing page**

The home page of your site is the most important, since it's the first one that viewers see. The home page should include an introduction to you and your books.

Many authors are choosing to go with one-page sites, which are easy to load and view on a cell phone or tablet. If you choose to produce a one-page site, be sure to include a bio, a description of the book or books (if you have multiple books, you'll probably want to set up individual pages for each one), a section featuring (or providing outside links to) news, events, or whatever content you've determined is valuable to your viewers, and contact information. If you're going to offer a newsletter or email access, be sure to include a spot for sign-ups on the landing page. Also, be sure to link to your social media sites and those sites where readers can purchase your books.

3. An "About the Author" or bio page
Most readers want to know more about the authors of their favorite books, so be sure to provide information about yourself. Be generous with this info--most readers will have already read the bio that appears on the jacket of your book, so be sure to offer more in the way of information or insight into you and your writing process. If you cover this kind of information in your blog, be sure to point that out to viewers, so that they can go there to learn more about you, too.

4. A place where visitors can locate information that has value
Once you've determined the goal for your website, you'll want to provide whatever information feeds that goal and provides value to your viewers. You

might include items that contain content relevant to your book or its genre, information about new developments related to the book or its contents, updates about events or appearances, and general information your audience might find interesting. Remember, your website has to somehow help your viewers--either by teaching them something new, by providing them with resources to gain more information, or by entertaining them. Give them something at your site that they cannot find elsewhere, and you'll have them visiting often.

5. **Testimonials**
Sometimes readers visit websites because they're considering buying a book (this is often true for readers) or they want to learn more about you and your platform (more likely for media folks, publicists, and venue hosts that are considering having you appear for an event). To help those looking for this kind of information, be sure to include testimonials from readers and others who can help present you and your work in the best light. If possible, include photographs of those who provide testimonials--the visuals have much more impact than just the printed testimony and will help lend authenticity to testimonial statements.

6. **A place to announce news (awards, new releases, new editions, etc.)**
If you or your books have won awards, if you have a new release coming out, or if there is general news about your books (e.g., a new edition, a new

publisher, or a sale event), be sure to include that information somewhere on your website.

7. Links to social media sites
Once you have a website that provides value to readers and other visitors, you'll want to make it as easy as possible for them to share your website with one another. Be sure to include buttons that allow your readers to send links of your content and your site to popular social media sites, so that visitors can share your website with others who might be interested in the same content.

8. An invitation to sign up for newsletters and other mailings
If the goal for your website is to help build your platform, you'll want to be sure to include ways for visitors to sign up for newsletters or other sources of information that you provide. Most authors provide a Subscribe form somewhere on the site that allows visitors to sign up for these resources.

9. A contact page
Finally, think about how you'd like your audience to contact you. Some authors like having viewers reach them via email, while others prefer to use a contact form. Either method is fine; just be sure to provide some way for readers and general viewers to contact you if they have questions.

CHAPTER 25. GIVEAWAYS AND PROMOTIONAL ITEMS

When planning publicity budgets, authors should be sure to carve out room for the creation of promotional items (these include objects such as standing posters, bookmarks, magnets, printed bags, etc.) and for printing copies of the book to send to reviewers and fulfill giveaways.

Giveaways

Giveaways are important tools for obtaining reviews and can be a great way to expose potential readers to the content of your book. They're also used in contests and blog tours as ways of generating interest and response in an audience.

One of the best sources for running giveaways is Goodreads. Since Goodreads only allows authors to run giveaways for six months after a book's release date, it's important to take advantage of that opportunity and schedule as many giveaways as possible during that window of time. I recommend offering ten copies for each giveaway and running the giveaways for two months each time you hold one. Once each giveaway is over, Goodreads will send you a list of winners, and you'll then mail them hard copies of your book (no ebooks are allowed in these giveaways). The idea is that the people who win the giveaway will write a review on Goodreads, which is helpful for other readers looking for books like yours.

If you plan to schedule a blog tour, it will be important to offer both print and ebook options to bloggers for giveaways they may want to run when they post about your book. Many bloggers have worldwide followers, so consider offering print copies for local readers and ebook copies for those in the rest of the world. For US authors, for example, I recommend offering one or two print copies to readers in the United States and Canada, and the same number of copies of ebook versions to the giveaway winners in other countries.

It's also important to remember to have your ebook ready in both epub and MOBI formats, since many ebook readers use different platforms for reading. Most bloggers will host the giveaway via embedded platforms like Rafflecopter and will notify the author when they have a list of winners for the giveaway. It is up to the author to send those copies to the winners, so be prepared to email ebooks and pay for postage when fulfilling print copies of giveaway wins.

Giveaways also provide an excellent way to increase your social media presence. In exchange for an entry into your giveaway, you can ask readers for something in return, including writing a review on Amazon.com or Goodreads; posting about your book on Twitter or Facebook; following you on Twitter, Facebook, or Instagram; signing up for newsletter and email updates; or referring friends to your Amazon page, website, or blog.

It's important to have a goal in mind with each giveaway, since doing so will allow you to better design the giveaway. For example, if your main goal is to build your presence on Twitter, you can ask a reader to tweet about your book as a requirement to enter the giveaway, and then use the other social media platforms (Goodreads, Facebook, Pinterest, email subscriptions, etc.) as bonus entry methods.

Promotional Items
Authors should plan to have some basic display items created for their books, especially if they plan to do book signings or speaking events. It's important to have signage at an event, both to notify those in the vicinity that an event is happening and also to promote the event before it occurs. For those authors who plan to give presentations at signings and speaking events, I recommend creating standing posters of their books. These are usually prepared by reprographics companies and they typically consist of a poster of the front cover of the book mounted on foam core, with a folding easel back to allow the poster to be free-standing. If the author is going to be speaking outdoors, it's often good to have the posters laminated to protect them from getting wet. The color will run on a poster that isn't laminated--I've had my own posters damaged by rain and people spilling drinks on them, so lamination is often worth the cost.

In terms of sizing standing posters, you want to think about how they'll be used. For bookstore window displays and outdoor events where you may want your sign to be seen from far-away, a larger poster (24 x 16 inches) may be appropriate. You might also want to create smaller sizes (18 x 12 inches, for example) for use on a table. Also, think about creating smaller-sized posters that will fit in your suitcase, which can help save costs on shipping when traveling to events.

It's also important to have items that prospective readers can take with them when they meet you at an event. Many authors produce bookmarks as promotional items (bookstores and libraries are always happy to hand these out for you, so print in large quantities and share them wherever you go). If printed bookmarks are too expensive, consider producing low-cost business cards as bookmarks (put the book's front cover image on one side of the business card, and ordering information on the back).

But bookmarks aren't the only type of promotional items–try to be as creative and unique as possible when deciding what kind of giveaways to offer and consider creating items that are inexpensive to produce, useful to readers, and that tie into your story in some way. Consider your target readers; what would they have a real use for that relates to your book? And is there an aspect of your book that can be translated into a useful or memorable item that would be useful to a reader? If so, try to create and purchase these items in large quantities, since that will help drive down the individual item price.

Be sure to hand out promotional items to anyone who approaches you at an event, in addition to making those items available in booths, on convention exhibit tables, in event gift bags, and as handouts wherever you appear.

Also consider selling themed merchandise on your website and at large events such as street fairs, trade shows, and conventions where you're appearing as a speaker or vendor. Create custom T-shirts, coffee mugs, e-reader covers, jewelry, framed art, and other such items, and have them available for sale on your website or at events. Businesses such as Vistaprint, CafePress, Zazzle, and MOO offer low-cost options for producing printed promotional items, business cards, and bookmarks.

It's always good to carry printed business cards to hand out at events. I recommend including the front cover image on one side (so plan to print four-color on at least one side) and your website, Amazon URL and other contact and ordering information for your readers on the reverse side.

If printing business cards and bookmarks is too expensive for your budget, consider printing out paper copies of your Q&A or press releases to use as handouts at events. You can place copies of these on the seats at book-signing and speaking events, and have them available on the table at book fairs or conventions. Whatever you can afford, try to have something you can give to a reader who might not be ready to buy at the moment, but who might consider it later (or pass it along to other readers) after having a chance to look over your promotional material.

CHAPTER 26. FINDING YOUR READING AUDIENCE

One of the biggest challenges for authors, especially those who are promoting their first book, can be identifying their reading audience.

For those who write genre fiction, the road can sometimes be a little easier than it is for other authors. Genres such as romance, erotica, fantasy, science fiction, mystery, and thriller are extremely popular, and there are many conventions, professional writing organizations, blogs, and events aimed at writers and readers of those books. Having outlets such as these provides authors of genre fiction some already established arenas for networking and marketing. And readers in some of these categories can be voracious--they will oftentimes seek out books in these categories on their own, without much prompting from authors.

But for those authors who don't write genre fiction, or who write nonfiction, finding readers can be a little more challenging. In those cases (and for genre fiction writers as well), I recommend using a number of determining factors--the Who, What, Where, Why, and How--to find your reading audience.

1. Determine *Who* Your Reading Audience Is
A good exercise for any author who has written a book is to take a moment to visualize the ideal reader for that book. Once that person is in mind, authors can then identify key attributes, or

demographics, that define that ideal reader. For example, would the ideal reader be male or female? Older or younger (or is age a factor at all)? Educated beyond high school? Affluent or not? Religious? Political? Of a certain cultural background? Concentrated in one region or country or worldwide? As authors begin to flesh out the characteristics of the reading audience, they will get a sense of what this ideal reader looks like in terms of measurable attributes.

2. **Determine** *What* **Motivates Your Reading Audience**

Once the demographics are determined, authors can then focus on the psychological motivators, or psychographics, of their reading audience. These can be indicators of what the ideal readers like, where they spend their free time, where they shop (especially for books), what media programs (television, radio, social media, etc.) the ideal readers frequent, etc. Psychographics can also include emotional indicators such as values, ideals, or political preferences; identifying these factors can help authors determine where they might find their audience spending their time and money.

For example, if your ideal readers are active or into health, they might frequent a gym or buy from stores like Whole Foods or Trader Joe's. They may be pet owners, or they may enjoy specific weekend activities such as hiking, yoga, walking, or eating out with friends. The more places authors can identify as the places where their ideal readers spend their time, the more the authors can identify possible arenas that might offer good opportunities for promotion in the way of advertising or appearances.

3. **Determine** *Where* **to Find Your Reading Audience**

Once authors have developed demographic and psychographic profiles of their readers, they'll have a better sense of where and how their readers spend their time and money. Knowing where they go to find books, for example, will help authors determine the best places to promote their work. Are your ideal readers likely to buy based on reviews, word-of-mouth recommendations from friends, or both? If the book is nonfiction, what problem does the book solve for your ideal readers, and what are the outcomes they are looking for? If your book is genre fiction, where would your ideal readers go to find that type of book?

For example, if an author's new romance novel falls into the chick lit genre, the author might decide that the ideal reader is a young woman between the ages of 18 and 35 who is a working professional. Since the ideal reader is young, chances are she spends time on social media like Twitter, Instagram, and Snapchat, and possibly dating sites like Tinder. If she is someone who is an affluent reader, perhaps she visits indie bookstores or purchases from Amazon. If she is less affluent, the author should think about approaching the local library to shelve the book for those readers who cannot afford to buy books.

4. Determine *Why* **Your Reading Audience Buys**
Once you have thought about the who, what, and where factors for your ideal readers, the next factor to consider is why your ideal readers are likely to purchase this particular book. Determining why readers choose a book involves taking a close look at what makes your book special or different from other books like it. Does your book focus on a special theme or cause that might appeal to your ideal readers? Is there a particular area of interest, such as a hobby, lifestyle, or subject of study that sets your book apart? Do your characters demonstrate interests or skills that might match those of your ideal readers? And is there an interesting premise, situation, or question that forms the central idea behind your book?

Once you know the special elements that characterize your book, you can identify individual experts and venues where your ideal readers might find information or sources on these items of special interest. These can include groups or organizations, businesses, bloggers, films or television shows, or even products that are used by people interested in the elements of your book that set it apart. Search for these experts and venues online using key words and include them in your promotional plans as possible ways to target members of your ideal reading audience.

It can also help to look at other books that are similar to yours. You can contact the authors for possible marketing collaboration or locate readers of these books through reviews on sites like Amazon.com and Goodreads.

5. Determine *How* Best to Connect with Your Reading Audience

Once you know your ideal readers, you need to reach out to them. But how? Many authors use social media as a way of connecting with readers, but it's important to make sure that the exchange in this case is focused on relationship-building, rather than selling your book.

You can also connect with potential readers by networking with friends, colleagues, and family members who may have similar interests and can introduce you to those who might become your ideal readers.

Once you've identified which venues your readers visit, try advertising or running promotional specials such as contests and giveaways at these locations. Speak, advertise, or hand out promotional items and copies of your book, and follow up with those who show interest or indicate they'd like to learn more about you or your writing, or both.

You can also attend speaking events, trade shows, book and street fairs, conferences, and conventions that your ideal readers frequent.

Be sure to interact on blogs your ideal readers visit and be sure to list your website, blog, and book information after your posts on those sites.

CHAPTER 27: DON'T FORGET TO FINISH YOUR SWING

As many of you know, I have a daughter who plays college softball. Thus, I spend most of my weekends in the spring driving for hours on California highways and sitting in the stands at college stadiums, cheering the team on while trying to avoid the inevitable sunburn and rear-end numbness we softball moms lovingly refer to as "bleacher butt." Yes, it can be tiring and time-consuming, but the end result is worth it--I get to watch my daughter and her teammates play the game they love, and nothing gives me more joy (except maybe, after a few nights spent on lumpy hotel mattresses, coming home and sleeping in my own bed).

While I don't purport to know a lot about softball--I never played it, although I did play a season of women's rugby in college and have the dental work to prove it--I've learned some invaluable lessons from this sport that my daughter adores. One lesson in particular that resonates is the adage to "finish your swing," which my daughter's hitting coaches claim is the most important part of sending that softball over the fence for a home run. And just as in softball, finishing strong can be the best way to guarantee success for authors who are trying to promote their books.

As a publicist, I've been hired by many authors who are eager to succeed at the publicity game. They are willing to pay me for my services, travel to parts unknown to give talks and sign books, and spend lots of money on printing, postage, and other expenses to get the word out about their work. But while the majority of the authors are willing to part with their hard-earned cash, I find that oftentimes they don't consider the fact that the work of promotion isn't finished once I'm able to garner whatever type of publicity they're looking for, whether it's setting up a book or blog tour, helping them place articles in magazines and journals, or scheduling media interviews.

And that's because making these types of events happen is not all there is to it. Once an event or interview is set up, there's a lot more work to be done--booksellers want display copies, giveaways, and sometimes even food and drinks supplied for their events, and most of them expect the author to fill the seats with attendees. Likewise, other venues where authors appear, whether it be a library, a museum, a church, a specialty store, or a professional organization luncheon, often hold the same expectations. And even bloggers expect review and giveaway copies, along with the promise that the author will share the blogger's link on social media sites.

This means that authors have a continued role to play once their publicists book gigs for them. Yes, getting the bookseller, producer, or venue host to say yes is the first step (and oftentimes a big one, depending on the importance of the event to the author), and yes, some events, blog posts, and interviews bring their own viewers. But in most cases, the work isn't finished with the confirmation. In addition to showing up (which requires a certain amount of preparation in itself), authors can expect to provide all the amenities for the event including, in many cases, the attendees.

But it's not fair, authors say--I have to write the book, hire a publicist, pay a lot of expenses, and then I'm supposed to fill the room, too?

The answer is a resounding yes--your publicist and the venue host can do a good portion of the promoting legwork for you, but in general, the events your publicist sets up for you will only be successful if *you* follow through.

"But where do I find people to attend my events?" authors ask. Many authors are reluctant to go back to their friends and family members who have already been asked multiple times to buy books and attend signings. But there are other ways to promote an event; here are some to consider:

• Think outside the friends and family box--post notices at work, school, church, and book clubs. Hand them out to your fellow yoga classmates, post them at the grocery store and coffee shop near you, and keep them handy when traveling, so you always have one to give to a potential attendee

- Offer incentives for people to come--free food and drinks and giveaways can often be a motivator for those who are considering attending an event
- Place notices in local media online calendars
- Send out press releases to local media and schedule interviews prior to the event
- Announce events on social media sites
- Blog about your upcoming events--share some insights into what you plan to do there or what the event means to you
- Promote your event or interview at related group meetings and on social media sites where you and your books' content would be of interest
- List event dates and times prominently on your blog and website
- Send out reminders to those on your email lists
- Be proactive in promoting--tell anyone who might be interested, as often as possible, about your upcoming appearances, interviews, and events

While completing these activities might sound daunting, consider the ramifications of not doing any social media promotion, not sending display and review copies, not providing giveaways on blog tours, not listing events on your blog and website, and not talking about your upcoming gigs to anyone who might be interested. Without these types of author follow-up, your events run the risk of not being very successful. You might have connected by setting up the event, but the real power is in the follow-through. Ask my daughter--she's hitting over .400 this season, and she'll be the first to tell you that even though her swing is strong, the really big hits don't come unless she finishes moving that bat all the way through.

CHAPTER 28. THE IMPORTANCE OF GRATITUDE

In my many years as a book publicist, I've worked with clients, media specialists, producers, editors, graphic designers, booksellers, conference organizers, and publishing experts. In all of my interactions, I've found that the most important step to my success in any of these relationships has been to express gratitude for what they have done for me. Whether it is thanking my clients for their business, following up a book signing by thanking a bookseller for her effort in setting up the event, or sending a thank you note to a producer for giving a client an interview, there is nothing more important than being grateful for the time and energy that person spent in helping me to promote my client.

Although this would seem obvious to some, many of us don't take the time to thank those we work with. But in the publicity business, so much of what is granted to me and my clients stems from me making a request--to a bookseller, a distributor, a blogger, or a journalist--for something that is going to help get the word out about my client and the new book. None of these people have to say *yes* to my queries, so when they do, I'm extremely grateful and try my best to let them know it.

If I have one final word of advice for authors who are planning to do some publicity work for their books, it would be to approach their promotional efforts with a feeling of gratitude. In the course of asking others to help spread the word about their books, authors will find that they get more *yes*es and keep those connections longer if they express their appreciation and thanks to those who have allowed them opportunities to speak about, advertise, promote, and publicize their work.

It's easy in today's world to become so busy with the tasks before us that we lose sight of how we accomplish those tasks. In most cases, it is often through the generosity and effort put out by others that we are able to be successful. Make it a habit to give thanks frequently and often, and you will realize much success in your journey to promote your work.

Chapter 29. Straight Talk on Book Publicity Costs

The question I hear most often from writers these days is a simple one: What should an author expect to pay for a typical book promotion campaign?

The answer is equally simple: It depends. Different public relations agencies will charge different fees, so costs will vary depending on the type of publicist you decide to hire. Some agencies charge monthly retainer fees that can typically range in the thousands of dollars. Others have established hourly rates or will create a contract for a set amount of work and charge accordingly.

As an independent public relations specialist, I work one-on-one with clients directly and usually only handle one or two clients at a time. I like to meet with my clients to go over their requirements, and the extent of my services is determined by what they want in the way of publicity. Some just want a press release or limited media coverage for a one-day event; others want speaking engagements, a book tour, a blog tour, radio and TV coverage, and more. I charge $50 per hour, and usually work about ten to fifteen hours per week for each of my clients. I've had clients who contract for as little as five hours of work, and others whom I work with for several months. I keep detailed time sheets that I send out every two weeks, and I always do only what clients have contracted with me to do. Many of my authors are self-published, although I have an equal number who have published with larger houses and want to do a little more than what's covered in their publisher's publicity contract.

Many writers also ask about success rates for promoting self-published books. I've been pretty successful with self-published authors. For example, one of my clients, Pamela Fagan Hutchins, has become an indie sensation with her *What Doesn't Kill You* romantic mystery series.

When Pamela and I first worked together, she had written five nonfiction books, but had never tried her hand at fiction. She hired me to help promote her first *What Doesn't Kill You* novel, *Saving Grace*, which became a Number 1 best seller in the romantic mystery category and Number 34 overall on Amazon. She followed *Saving Grace* with the nonfiction self-publishing guide, *What Kind of Loser Indie Publishes, and How Can I Be One Too?* and a series of romantic mystery novels featuring her *Saving Grace* characters.

We scheduled a number of book signings and media interviews for Pamela to start off her publicity efforts for *Saving Grace*, and those helped generate some initial buzz about her work. Then she really jump-started her sales with a sixty-city tour of the United States that she did the first summer after the book launched. Pamela bought a mobile home and, along with her one-eyed Boston terrier, Petey, traveled the country holding book signings at bookstores, libraries, RV parks, and any other venue where she'd be allowed to speak. She and her husband Eric took a second trip the following summer visiting a grand total of forty-six states to help promote her new books, and her sales soared into the thousands. Now an Amazon best-selling author, Pamela speaks at writing, romance, and mystery conferences across the country. You can learn more about Pamela and her books at www.pamelafaganhutchins.com and her publishing company, SkipJack Publishing, at www.skipjackpublishing.com.

But even those who can't afford cross-country book tours can still do a lot with a little publicity. I recommend that most authors at least have a professional press release done, and do some book signings, even if they're local. In addition to creating buzz and making personal contacts with readers, authors can get some additional mileage out of those events by getting their books stocked in the store and placing photos from the signing on their websites. I also think a blog tour is a relatively easy way to get noticed, although it can be time-consuming to set up (I research appropriate bloggers and their sites, and then contact them directly regarding participation in the tour).

As a publicist, the main task I accomplish for my clients is the phone work--I am persistent in encouraging media, bookstore, and other venue representatives to look at the work done by my authors. And I think that objectivity is what convinces them to say yes to an event date. It's hard for an author to call a radio producer or bookstore owner to pitch his or her own book, but when I call and say a client's work is great, the producers and store managers listen. And I'm persistent, which is key. It's often easy for people to say no, so I keep going back with new angles and approaches until I get them to say yes (this can be the time-consuming part, but it works!).

When you're ready to hire a publicist, be sure to check out a lot of agencies and individual consultants and find one with the right attitude and fit for you and your work. And don't be afraid to ask for references--good public relations professionals should always be willing to put you in touch with their clients so you can hear firsthand what they have to say about the publicists' professionalism, follow-through, and success rates.

CHAPTER 30. WHEN IS IT TIME TO HIRE A PUBLICIST?

As soon as a book is published (or sometimes sooner), many authors--especially first-timers-- believe that hiring a publicist is the first step on the promotional to-do list.

But is it? Should all authors hire publicists?

You'd think, since I'm a publicist, I'd be the first to say yes. But before you hire a publicist, please consider the following:

1. **Public relations, or publicity, is just one aspect of promoting a book**

Many authors assume that in addition to promoting the author and the book to the media, publicists will also issue daily tweets, upload Facebook and blog posts, take care of marketing the book on social cataloguing websites, handle distribution issues, create and place paid advertisements, send in contest entries, mail out copies to reviewers, set up blog tours, schedule signing events, and more. While many publicists have branched out and do handle some of these tasks, a number of them don't.

Traditionally, publicists create press releases and media kits, handle media inquiries, and pitch their clients' work (or the clients) to print, radio, television, and Internet media representatives, including producers, editors, and reporters. Publicists also assist their clients with interviews and event appearances and (in the case of celebrities or better-known authors) can help with damage control when public images become tarnished.

Some publicists have become adept at doing more than just media work and offer additional services, such as booking speaking engagements or setting up blog tours. But the majority of the publicists out there are focused on media relations. For this reason, authors shouldn't assume that a publicist is trained or interested in handling all aspects of marketing; publicity is just one part of marketing, and many publicists specialize in media work and nothing else.

2. Not every author has a platform or book that is promotable

Many readers will shudder at the audacity of item 2 here, but it's necessary to speak this truth. Not all authors have developed their platforms enough (in fact, some have no platform at all) to be worthy of attention from the media. And not all books (brace yourself here) are written or edited well enough to merit media coverage.

In order to be of interest to the media, an author or the book *must be newsworthy*; i.e., the author must have some specialty or area of expertise that is interesting to a news producer or editor, or the book must cover a topic that is relevant and newsworthy to a media audience. Before rushing out to hire publicists, authors need to first do a little honest soul-searching and ask themselves, "Do I have specialized expertise or some type of compelling experience that is news? Does my book cover a topic that is in the news right now? Am I or is my book (or a combination of both) truly newsworthy?" If an author can answer yes to any of these questions, then the next question (and this one can be much harder to answer) is: "How so?"

If you can't answer these questions (or you aren't sure that the media outlets you'd like to approach would consider you or your book news), then perhaps it isn't time to hire a publicist. This is often the case with first-time authors, who haven't yet developed a track record with readers or haven't yet created a unique and memorable brand for themselves.

Instead, those who need to develop a platform should probably work on that first. How? By creating and maintaining meaningful social nctworks, developing a following of dedicated readers (which might mean writing more than one book), creating a brand or image within a specific genre, developing a reputation as an expert through teaching, speaking, or writing articles, and similar work. Then, once there is something of interest to offer media outlets, consider finding someone to help with exposure.

3. Even with a compelling platform or a book that is somehow newsworthy, there is no guarantee that a publicist will be able to obtain media exposure

This fact might be surprising to some, but here's the honest truth: hiring a publicist does not automatically guarantee coverage in the media. An author can have a compelling background, and the book can touch on a topic that the author and publicist consider a hot news item, and still not get media coverage. Authors need to remember that producers and editors (along with book bloggers, book reviewers, and contest judges) are inundated with queries about authors and their books every day. So, even if there is a story there, and your publicist does a good job of pitching it, there is no guarantee that a media representative will be interested, or hasn't seen or heard that story before. It may be a good story, but timing, saturation, deadlines, space issues, and a host of other reasons can cause even a good pitch to be ignored or refused.

Being passed over by a producer or editor doesn't mean that the author hasn't written a good book or doesn't have a great platform (or that the publicist isn't doing a good job). What it means is that coverage in the news is a tricky--and sometimes serendipitous--business. A publicist cannot force a media representative to like a pitch about an author or a book. The reporter, producer, or editor who hears the pitch has to decide if it's a story that a) can be used, b) will interest the audience, and c) hasn't been covered already by that particular (or any other) media outlet. Of course, there is no way to know if an editor will say yes to feature coverage, but authors should realize that even if their platforms and stories are good, they will sometimes (more often than not, in some cases) hear a no.

4. **It sounds good, until the first interview**

I can't tell you the number of clients (okay, I can, but I won't) who have hired me to handle publicity for them and then panic as soon as the interview requests come rolling in. If you hire a publicist, then you have to expect that you're going to be in the public eye, which may include speaking engagements and interviews. If you're uncomfortable in front of a camera, a microphone, or a live audience, then hiring a publicist could be problematic. Yes, you can ask your publicist to only obtain online or print interviews for you, but that might limit how much exposure you allow yourself. In general, you can bank on the fact that, if you and your book are newsworthy, a publicist is going to help you to be seen in the public eye--and that usually includes public appearances and radio and television interviews.

5. **Publicity costs money that you may not have budgeted**

Many authors become so wrapped up in the aspects of writing and publishing their books that they forget that marketing the book will require some capital. Generally, most publicists charge a monthly retainer or, like me, work on an hourly basis. It's a good idea to shop around and see what agencies and individual book publicists are charging, so that you have a clear idea of what a publicity campaign might cost. It's also important to know what kind of publicity you're looking for and how much you'd like to spend on that aspect of your marketing budget before you contact a publicist, so that you can ensure that there is a good fit between you and the professional you'd like to hire.

So, now that I've discussed caveats to consider before hiring a publicist, when is it ideal to do so?

The best time to hire a publicist is when . . .

1. You have a well-written, professionally designed and edited book, and its contents are somehow newsworthy.

2. Your book is set up for distribution in both online and print versions.

3. You have a platform that is newsworthy.

4. You have a clearly distinguishable brand image for you and/or your book that is newsworthy.

5. You have a clearly defined genre and audience (your book may fit into more than one category and appeal to more than one audience; if so, that's good--just be sure you can articulate them to your publicist when you're ready to hire).

6. You are comfortable with being in the public eye and are committed to making appearances once they're booked.

7. You have a budget for publicity.

8. You are willing to trust your publicist's expertise and let your publicist do his or her job.

Once you feel you and your book are ready, pay attention to what your potential publicist requests from you in the way of information. Most will want to read the book first and discuss with you what you're looking for in the way of publicity, so be ready to provide that information. Network with other authors for recommendations on publicists they've worked with who might be a good fit for you and your book, and always ask for references before you hire.

CHAPTER 31. THE TEN BEST BOOKS ON WRITING

You're probably wondering why is there a chapter about books on writing in a guidebook devoted to publicity.

But remember, this is a guide to *book* publicity. And, as I point out in Chapter 2, writing a good book is the most important task you'll face as an author who plans to promote a book.

Thus, I've listed here the experts I've turned to whenever I've found myself in one of those middle-of-the-project writing funks. These books, on how to maneuver through the alternately frustrating and fulfilling maze of fiction (and in some cases nonfiction) writing, line the shelves in my office. Although I've read dozens of them over the years, a select few have made their way to a place of honor on the shelf reserved for those books I refuse to give away. I know that many writers will have other worthy contenders on their lists; these are mine, in reverse order:

10. *Writing Down the Bones* by Natalie Goldberg

I had trouble picking a tenth book, because there are so many others that deserve to be on this list and aren't (I considered Burroway's *Writing Fiction: A Guide to Narrative Craft*, Forster's *Aspects of the Novel*, Olen Butler's *From Where You Dream: The Process of Writing Fiction*, DeMarco-Barrett's *Pen on Fire*, and more). But this one made the list because it has remained on my shelf for over a decade and its short and simple chapters, aimed mostly at beginning writers, speak truth. From "Beginner's Mind" to "Rereading and Rewriting," each pithy and instructive section reminds us what we already know. We read Natalie Goldberg and, no matter where we are on our respective writing journeys, we learn.

9. *20 Master Plots and How to Build Them* by **Ronald B. Tobias**

I have returned to this book countless times to remind myself a) that writers have been telling stories for centuries, and b) that the best stories have form. The form of a novel can be as simple as a beginning, middle, and end, or it can follow the patterns of quest, revenge, pursuit, maturation, sacrifice, and discovery. Tobias reminds us that though there are hundreds of plot variations out there, a few of those structures have become classics, loved by readers everywhere. It is to those that we aspire.

8. *The 38 Most Common Fiction Writing Mistakes (and How to Avoid Them)* by **Jack M. Bickham**

I loved this book from the moment I opened its cover. There's nothing fancy in Bickham's style--he grabs us by the neck and instructs us in each direct and wonderful chapter on what we should and shouldn't do when writing. The chapter "Don't Warm Up Your Engines" provides one of the best explanations I've read on where a story should start. When Bickham speaks, it behooves us to listen.

7. *Zen in the Art of Writing* by **Ray Bradbury**

I heard Ray Bradbury speak one year at the Santa Barbara Writers Conference, and I'll never forget the amazing zeal and spunkiness of this fiction-writing legend. Bradbury brings the same energy and outspokenness to *Zen in the Art of Writing* as he does to his own classic tales. He describes his early years trying to eke out a living as a young writer with a family and then urges writers to stick to it and to do it with love. "Let the world burn through you," he says. In the Zen world of fiction writing, Bradbury is a warrior-king.

6. *Writing Begins with the Breath: Embodying Your Authentic Voice* by **Laraine Herring**

This is one of my most recent acquisitions, but it quickly found a home on my shelf of favorites. I took it with me on a writing residency and only allowed myself to read one chapter a day, doling them out one-by-one so I could immerse myself in each section's quiet relevance. The book is divided into three parts: "Focusing the Mind," "The Deep Writing Process," and "Embracing What and Where You Are." *Writing Begins with the Breath* both illuminates and gently instructs, and the imaginative exercises called "Touchstones" at the end of each chapter make us pause, reflect, and return to this book again and again.

5. *Bird by Bird: Some Instructions on Writing and Life* by **Anne Lamott**

What hasn't been said about this book? It's a classic, and Anne Lamott has become a well-deserved fixture on the writing circuit and in composition classrooms all over the world because of this gifted text. As she says in the opening, good writing is about telling the truth, and she has done that, taking us from "shitty first drafts" to publication and deftly addressing everything in-between. Honest, inspirational, and very real, Anne Lamott illuminates the writing process in a way that is both accessible and revealing, telling the truth about writing so vividly that reading her words is like coming home.

4. *On Writing: A Memoir of the Craft* by Stephen King

Who would have thought that a memoir by one of the world's best-selling authors could so expertly define the practical facets of the writing process? In *On Writing*, Stephen King not only openly (and in some cases, with heart-wrenching candor) describes his own experiences as a professional writer struggling with personal demons, but he also shares his passion and knowledge about what makes writing good. My favorite section has to do with revision; in it, King tells the story about a piece of fiction he wrote in high school and submitted to a magazine editor. The editor wrote back: "*Not bad, but PUFFY. You need to revise for length. Formula: 2nd Draft = 1st Draft–10%. Good luck.*" King says that this piece of advice changed the way he rewrote his fiction "once and forever." Thanks to Stephen King, it has changed ours, too.

3. *How to Write a Damn Good Novel* by James N. Frey

I lent this book to a member of my writing group, and one of his dogs got to it and chewed through half of the front cover. I have to laugh every time I lift it off the shelf (it gives a whole new meaning to the term "dog-eared"!). But I love this book for its intensity and no-nonsense focus on what makes a novel good. Frey gives the best advice I know on how to create unforgettable characters, infuse a plot with conflict, and write dialogue that sings. I come back to this book often for the solid, sensible advice that fills its pages.

2. *The Joy of Writing Sex: A Guide for Fiction Writers* by Elizabeth Benedict

I don't know how this became my number two all-time favorite, but perhaps it's because I (ahem) have trouble writing about sex. I use my Catholic upbringing as my excuse; for some reason, I imagine the nuns at my elementary and high schools peering over my shoulder every time I write a love scene. But whether it's my own modesty, or the fear that the intimacy my characters display on the page will reveal more about me than it does them, writing sex scenes--good sex scenes--is really difficult. All of that changed, however, after I found Benedict's book, which provides insight and advice on how to not only make sex scenes convincing, but also how to use them to reveal character and create and/or resolve conflict. Benedict uses wonderful examples from some of the most respected writers to illustrate the dramatic impact of a well-written sex scene.

And she addresses it all--married sex, adulterous sex, illicit sex--in a way that is fresh, revealing, and inspiring. So whenever those nuns appear, I reach for this book and let this classic guide remind me that it's okay for sex to be part of the story.

And, drum roll please . . .

1. *Writing the Breakout Novel* by **Donald Maass**

My husband bought me this book for Christmas the first year I started writing fiction and it has become my all-time favorite writing guide. I've turned to it so often that the pages are covered with sticky notes, highlighted passages, fingerprints, and coffee stains. The book is designed for mid-list authors looking for a way to move ahead in the industry, but the advice packed within its pages is useful for beginners as well. For a book to be a breakout success, Maass says, it must have the following: an original premise, high stakes, a strong sense of time and place, and larger-than-life characters. And Maass, a literary agent and author of seventeen novels, knows whereof he speaks. I was fortunate enough to attend one of his seminars, where we used some of the draft exercises that became part of his *Writing the Breakout Novel Workbook*. Both the original book and the workbook are essential instruments in any writer's toolkit, but if I was going to be sent to a desert island and could only take one book on writing with me, *Writing the Breakout Novel* is the one I would pack in my suitcase.

And, okay, one more . . . (because I find I can never limit myself to just ten):

Big Magic: Creative Living Beyond Fear by Elizabeth Gilbert

In this wonderful book, renowned *Eat, Pray, Love* author Elizabeth Gilbert grants authors and artists the permission to create free of fear or, in many cases, in concert with it. Especially noteworthy are the early sections on the distinction between being a genius and having genius pour through you (and how the latter reflects the true nature of the artist), and how ideas can get sidetracked and, if they're set aside too long, lost. Gilbert argues that even if these ideas elude you, they often appear elsewhere, pursued by others in a concept known as multiple discovery. Fascinating and liberating, this book celebrates the joy of creating, and gifts all authors and artistic types with the knowledge that it's okay to just do the work, no matter the experience level or eventual outcome. A magical and inspiring read, not just for authors, but for anyone who yearns to be a creative explorer.

CHAPTER 32. PUBLISHING RESOURCES

Here is a brief list of some of my favorite sources for information on book publishing:

Creativity:

Brain Pickings https://www.brainpickings.org/

Cover Design:

Troy O'Brien   http://www.obriendesign.biz/

Editing:

Jodie Renner   http://www.jodierennerediting.com/
Erin Willard   http://erincopyeditor.com/

General Publishing Resources:

Jon Kremer   http://www.bookmarket.com/

Indie Publishing:

Jane Friedman https://janefriedman.com/
JA Konrath   http://jakonrath.com/
Bob Mayer   http://www.bobmayer.org/
Joanna Penn   http://www.thecreativepenn.com/

Acknowledgments

I would like to thank the following people for their help with this book:

First, a big shout-out to my beta readers, Ona Russell, Mary Vensel White, and Gregory A. Fournier. Without their keen insights and wise suggestions, many important sections in this book would not exist.

I am most grateful to Bill Kenower, Michael Steven Gregory, and Marni Freedman for their kind comments about the book and their continued support of me and my work.

I'd also like to thank my editor, Erin Willard, for her eagle-eyed copyediting and content suggestions. She is a true professional and my most trusted writing confidante. I value her wisdom and observations, which always make my work better.

Much appreciation also to my patient and talented graphic artist, Troy O'Brien, and to publishing gurus Devin and Moana Whipple, whose technical expertise is beyond compare.

Finally, many thanks and much love to my husband, Dan, and my children, Max and Sasha, who are always there for me, no matter what I do.

ABOUT THE AUTHOR

Paula Margulies is an author and the owner of Paula Margulies Communications, a public relations firm for authors and artists. She has received numerous awards for her short stories, essays, and novels, including her first novel, *Coyote Heart*, her short story collection, *Face Value: Collected Stories*, and her historical novel, *Favorite Daughter, Part One*. Margulies is a contributor to *Author Magazine*, the *San Diego Examiner,* and *The Writers Edge* (http://writersedgeinfo.blogspot.com) and has been awarded artist residencies at Caldera, Red Cinder Artist Colony, the Vermont Studio Center, and Centrum. Margulies resides in San Diego, California. For more information, please visit www.paulamargulies.com.

Dear Reader,

Thank you so much for taking the time to read *The Tao of Book Publicity: A Beginner's Guide to Book Promotion*. I hope it will act as a useful guide as you make plans to publicize your book(s).

I appreciate that you've spent your valuable time reading this book. If you found it helpful, please consider leaving a review at Amazon.com, Goodreads, or your favorite online retailer.

If you would like to know more about my writing or my work as a book publicist, please visit my website at http://www.paulamargulies.com.

Best wishes and happy marketing!
Paula Margulies

www.ingramcontent.com/pod-product-compliance
Lightning Source LLC
Chambersburg PA
CBHW021342290326
41933CB00037B/335